Disrupting the Future

Great Ideas for Creating a Much Better World

Edited by
Wayne Visser

Foreword by
Jorgen Randers

With contributions by

Dag Andersen, Iulie Aslaksen, Ugo Bardi, Catherine Cameron, John Elkington, Per Arild Garnåsjordet, Thomas N. Gladwin, Ulrich Golüke, Rob Gray, Carlos Joly, Alan Knight, Erling Moxnes, Terje Osmundsen, Thymio Papayannis, Jorgen Randers, Rasmus Reinvang, Nick Robins, Harald Siem, Chris Tuppen, Wayne Visser, Mathis Wackernagel, Karl Wagner, Peter Willis, and Philippe Zaouati

DISRUPTING THE FUTURE

Paperback edition first published in 2014
by Kaleidoscope Futures
68 Britten Close, London NW11 7HW

Copyright © 2014 Wayne Visser

All rights reserved. No part of this publication may be reproduced, stored in a retrieval system, or transmitted, in any form or by any means, electronic, mechanical, photocopying, recording or otherwise, except as permitted by the UK Copyright, Designs and Patents Act 1988, without the prior permission of the publisher.

Cover design by Wayne Visser and Kaleidoscope Futures Ltd. 2052 image adapted from 2052: *A Global Forecast for the Next Forty Years* (Jorgen Randers, Chelsea Green).

ISBN 978-1-908875-13-6

GREAT IDEAS FOR CREATING A MUCH BETTER WORLD

Contents

Preface	5
Foreword	6
Jorgen Randers	6
A Revolutionary Competition: Over Unity Free Energy	8
Dag Andersen	8
JM Keynes – An Ecological Economist? Multipliers and Morality	10
Iulie Aslaksen and Per Arild Garnåsjordet	10
The Sower's Strategy: A Way to Speed up the Energy Transition	15
Ugo Bardi	15
2052 for Prospectors	20
Catherine Cameron	20
The Gaia Prize For Fertile Failures	22
John Elkington	22
Rising Individualism Among the Young: A Great Challenge for Environmental Policy	24
Per Arild Garnåsjordet and Iulie Aslaksen	24
Massive Mind-shifting for Sustainability	28
Thomas N. Gladwin	28
Free Will is Highly Overrated	34
Ulrich Golüke	34
Scorecard of Organisational Un-sustainability	38
Rob Gray	38
EC Legislation to Regulate Financial Indexes	41
Philippe Zaouati and Carlos Joly	41
Gone Surfing	46
Alan Knight	46
MOOCs Bachelor in Sustainable Development	50
Erling Moxnes	50

Disrupting the Future

A Floor Tariff for Renewables in Least Developed Countries — 53
Terje Osmundsen — 53

Collaboration Among Mediterranean Islands — 57
Thymio Papayannis — 57

Compulsory Vacation: Reducing the Human Ecological Footprint Through More Annual Leave — 61
Jorgen Randers — 61

The 5-Year Global Sustainability Olympics: A Vision From the Future — 67
Rasmus Reinvang — 67

Finance 2050: Greening Financial Regulation — 72
Nick Robins and Catherine Cameron — 72

Population Scenarios for 2052 and Beyond: Dramatic Decline? — 75
Harald Siem — 75

Longer Life Products — 78
Chris Tuppen — 78

Strategies for Resilience: Before You Save the World, Prepare to Save Yourself — 84
Wayne Visser — 84

Ballyhoo Economic Risks of Overshoot — 88
Mathis Wackernagel — 88

Addressing the Underlying Systemic Issues — 93
Karl Wagner — 93

The Soil Carbon Olympics — 99
Peter Willis — 99

Preface

In *2052: A Global Forecast for the Next 40 Years* (Chelsea Green, 2012), Jorgen Randers draws on his own experience in the sustainability area, global forecasting tools, and the predictions – included in the book as 'Glimpses' – of more than thirty leading scientists, economists, futurists, and other thinkers to guide us through the future he feels is most likely to emerge towards the middle of the century.

At a meeting of 25 of the 'Glimpse' authors in Cambridge in October 2013, each participant was invited to present a 'great idea' (or thought, or development or fact) that they believed could improve on world developments over the next forty years. Following the meeting, the authors were invited to submit a brief summary of their 'Great Idea', for compilation.

Disrupting the Future – Great ideas for Creating a Much Better Future is the result of this process and is a remarkable collection of ideas and proposals by a diverse set of thought-leaders, each of which has responded in their own creative way to Jorgen Randers' concluding challenge in 2052: 'Please help me make my forecast wrong. Together we could create a much better world.'

Foreword

Jorgen Randers

We live in an age where knowledge is ubiquitous. We can no longer cite ignorance for our lack of decisive action on global challenges like climate change and poverty. We understand the issues and we know what needs to be done to tackle them – from weaning off our addiction to fossil fuels and promoting a circular economy, to nurturing economic growth in the poor world and redistribution of wealth in the rich world. So why is progress so slow?

Our global dilemma is that democratic societies are struggling to reach consensus on how to mitigate the long-term impacts of our modern lifestyles. In a nutshell, democracy is only good at promoting actions that have a short-term advantage. We need disruptive change, but we are stuck with institutions that favour incremental approaches.

There are two sensible ways beyond this impasse. The first is to employ less democratic forms of governance, such as China's state-directed capitalism, although it is hard to see this gaining favour in the West. The second is to find solutions that have short-term benefits for voters, yet also have the intended long-term effect of reducing climate change and poverty.

To meet our global challenges, we do not need more scientific data but more imagination of better futures. We do not need more policy proposals but better communication of the benefits of regulation. We do not need more demonization of business but better market incentives to align short-term and long-term opportunities.

Disrupting the Future is a response to this call for improved imagination, communication and incentives. I welcome this collection of voices, all of whom have generously shared their innovative ideas for making my somewhat bleak 2052 forecast wrong!

A Revolutionary Competition: Over Unity Free Energy

Dag Andersen

We are at a point in time where more of the same creates more problems than it solves. A problem cannot be solved by the same logic that created it, so we need a broader perspective, an expanded paradigm. In fact we need nothing less than a second Copernican-scale Revolution.

It is likely that this revolution will happen technologically – the new paradigm will probably get a breakthrough after physical evidence compels it forward. But it is very difficult for inventors, whose ideas blow apart the framework for established science and dogmas, to be taken seriously. Scientific dogmas create taboos, with the result that entire areas of research and enquiry are excluded from mainstream science and from regular sources of funding. There are also strong economic interests related to established technology, such as those supporting the oil industry.

Rupert Sheldrake has a suggestion, in his recent book *The Science Delusion: Freeing the Spirit of Enquiry* (2012), which I would support.

Many people claim to have made devices that produce 'free' energy using unconventional means. They claim their devices tap into the zero-point energy or quantum-vacuum field, drawing on unlimited reserves of free power. Others claim to have found new ways of using electrical and magnetic forces. A search on Internet for 'free energy devices' or 'over unity devices' gives thousands of hits. (The term 'over unity' refers to the ability of a machine to produce more energy than is put into it).

Sceptics claim that all these devices are impossible or fraudulent, and some of them may indeed be fraudulent. But, as Sheldrake asks, can we be sure that they all are? Perhaps some of these devices really work, and really can tap into new sources of energy.

Sheldrake's idea is that this is an area in which offering a prize might provide the best way forward. A prize for the most effective 'over unity' energy device might change the situation in energy research dramatically. He says, 'In fair tests, conducted in an open-minded spirit of enquiry, some devices may indeed produce more energy than is put into them from conventional sources. Or perhaps the contest will reveal that no such device exists, and no one will win the prize, giving scientific conservatives the pleasure of saying, "I told you so".'

The upside is sky high, the downside is very small and the process could be fun anyway, so, why not?

Dag Andersen (Norwegian, born 1947) is a political scientist, freelance advisor, lecturer, and author of The 5th Step: The Way to a New Society (2007).

JM Keynes – An Ecological Economist? Multipliers and Morality

Iulie Aslaksen and Per Arild Garnåsjordet

The visionary ideas of JM Keynes need to be re-established as a leading light in the global effort to solve the economic problem – to shift the world's focus from production to wellbeing. The understanding of society and public trust expressed by Keynes is urgently needed today as basis for collective action to solve the sustainability crisis.

By the provocative question – was JM Keynes an ecological economist and a leader of sustainability? – we encourage to Keynes to be re-read with an eye to his visionary ideas on public trust and collective action. We suggest resuscitating Keynes from a technocratic framework. When we were students and Keynesian economics was the prevalent approach, we learned about the arithmetical Keynes, in the context of multipliers for public expenditure. Nowhere did we learn about the moral Keynes with his concern for sustainability and questioning long-term economic growth.

On later reflection, we discovered the understanding of public trust embedded in Keynes' thinking and his idea for redirecting capital to improve society as a vision of sustainability. The time has come to re-establish the visionary ideas of Keynes in a global effort to solve the sustainability crisis – to shift the world's focus from production to wellbeing, within planetary boundaries. Restoring public trust is a fundamental condition for the macro-economy to function in its role of supporting the public good.

In his book, *The General Theory of Employment, Interest and Money* (1936), Keynes explains: 'It is the return of confidence, to speak in ordinary language, which is so insusceptible to control in an economy of individualistic capitalism. This is the aspect of the slump which bankers and business men have been right in emphasising, and which the economists who have put their faith in a "purely monetary" remedy have underestimated.'

During the unemployment crisis of the 1930s, Keynes realized that increased public spending was necessary to avoid a social disaster, but the increased spending was not supposed to last for a long time. His recommendation for public spending rested on a notion of public trust to ensure that economic balance would be established afterwards. Keynes argued that with income growth over a long period of time, the human mind would be induced to perceive high consumption as the ultimate goal – an end in itself rather than the means to a good life.

In his *Annual Report of the Arts Council 1945-1946*, Keynes envisaged that: 'The day is not far off when the economic problem will take the back seat where it belongs, and the arena of the heart and the head will be occupied, or reoccupied, by our real problems – the problems of life and of human relations, of creation and behavior and religion'.

In his vision of sustainability, Keynes was far ahead of his time, saying: 'When the accumulation of wealth is no longer of high social importance, there will be great changes in the code of morals ... The love of money as a possession – as distinguished from the love of money as a means to the enjoyments and realities of life – will be recognised for what it is, a somewhat disgusting morbidity ... But beware! ... For at least another hundred years we must pretend to ourselves and to everyone that fair is foul and foul is fair; for foul is useful and fair is not. Avarice and usury and precaution must be our gods a little longer still. For only they can lead us out of the tunnel of economic necessity into daylight.' (*The Future: Essays in Persuasion*, 1931).

Keynes also warned against the speculative economy, saying: 'It is generally agreed that casinos should, in the public interest, be inaccessible and expensive. And perhaps the same is true of Stock Exchanges (*The General Theory of Employment, Interest and Money*, 1936). The current financial crisis shows that the world has forgotten Keynes and does not have the public trust to stimulate the economy. In the United States, the Glass-Steagall legislation from 1933, which formed the basis for President Roosevelt's New Deal, was repealed in 1999.

The current crisis of unemployment calls for a revitalization of regulation of the financial sector. A problem for collective action is that the current crisis is framed either as pro-employment or pro-environment, but what is called for is a Green New Deal, a program for collective action to secure the common good, with regard to the environment as well as equity and employment. Society needs a vision for shared public values and strategies for collective action to protect them. The mission statement of the Green New Deal recalls Keynes' vision of sustainability: 'The Green New Deal will rekindle a vital sense of purpose, restoring public trust and refocusing the use of capital on public priorities and sustainability.'

Keynes is often misunderstood as a prophet of economic growth and excessive consumption since his message was to keep the economy running – in recession times. But Keynes was concerned that human weakness and greed would destroy nature and our livelihood, warning that: 'The same rule of self-destructive financial calculation governs every walk of life. We destroy the beauty of the countryside because the unappropriated splendours of nature have no economic value. We are capable of shutting off the sun and the stars because they do not pay a dividend.' (*National Self-Sufficiency*, 1933.). This is an ecological economist speaking – a philosopher of an ecological mindset.

Keynes' ideas contributed to President Roosevelt's New Deal for solving the unemployment crisis of the 1930s. The call for collective action embedded in Keynes' ideas reflects an understanding of society as having the ability to act in times of crisis. After World War II, Keynes' visions of redirecting funds to public priorities for the common good were put into practice in the rebuilding of society. Public funds were used in a context of public trust with the stated goal of improving society.

His ideas for a new Green New Deal are explored further at: http://www.greennewdealgroup.org/

Iulie Aslaksen is senior researcher in the research department of Statistics Norway and works with sustainability indicators, the Nature Index, and policy for sustainable development.

Per Arild Garnåsjordet (Norwegian, born 1945) is a geographer and senior researcher at Statistics Norway. From 1995–2006 he was managing director for Asplan Viak, a major consulting fim in urban and regional planning.

The Sower's Strategy: A Way to Speed up the Energy Transition

Ugo Bardi

'... and when he sowed, some seeds fell by the wayside, and the fowls came and devoured them up: some fell upon stony places, where they had not much earth and forthwith they sprung up, because they had no deepness of earth: and when the sun was up, they were scorched; and because they had no root, they withered away. And some fell among thorns; and the thorns sprung up, and choked them: but other fell into good ground, and brought forth fruit, some a hundredfold, some sixtyfold, some thirtyfold. Who hath ears to hear, let him hear.' (Matthew 13.4-9).

'Don't eat your seed corn!' is a well known saying. It refers to the age-old farmer's strategy of saving some of the harvest of the current year as seeds for the next. Unfortunately, however, our main energy source today, fossil fuels, produces no 'seeds'. Once extracted and used, it is gone forever and the same is true for all our mineral resources. This is what we call 'depletion'. In addition, fossil fuel burning is the main cause of climate change; an even more worrisome problem.

So far, we have been behaving like farmers who eat their seed corn; burning fossil fuels and consuming our resources as fast as possible. And we are still investing enormous amounts of money just to continue doing that. According to the Grantham Research Institute, about $650 billion were spent to develop new fossil fuel resources in 2012, mainly for oil and gas and, in particular, for the so called 'non conventional resources' (e.g. shale oil). This is the result of our current way of thinking, which emphasizes short-term gains. Not only does this strategy worsen the climate problem, but it forces us to spend more and more as depletion progresses and that perpetuates our dependence on fossil fuels. Obviously, that can't continue for a long time.

Is there a way out? Yes, if we go back to the wisdom of ancient farmers: don't eat your seed corn! Of course, we can't sow fossil fuels, but we can sow what these fuels provide: energy and minerals. We can use some of this energy and these minerals as seed to create the structures needed for a sustainable economy until, in the future, renewable energy eventually produces enough to replace itself and we learn how to recycle minerals much more efficiently than we do now. This is the sower's strategy applied to the modern world.

We are already using this strategy. At present, most of the resources used to build renewable energy plants and other elements of a sustainable economy come from fossil fuels. It is good that we are doing that, but are we doing enough? According to UNEP, some $250 billion were spent in 2012 for new renewable sources. This is much less than what is being invested in fossil energy but, so far, it has nevertheless allowed a rapid and consistent growth of renewable energy. The problem is that there is no guarantee that the necessary levels of investment will be maintained in the future if we continue giving priority to fossil fuels. Indeed, in 2012 we saw a decline in the investments in renewables. So, if we leave choices on energy to the market alone, we risk facing runaway climate change together with rapid resource depletion, without having sufficient resources available to create a new energy system. If we continue along this path we will eat all our seed corn.

Instead, we need to save our seed corn. This means investing a significant fraction of the energy and resources we are producing today into a sustainable economy, even though that may not provide the largest short-term returns. First, it means investing in renewable energy, i.e. energy technologies that don't produce greenhouse gases, are efficient in terms of 'energy return for energy invested' (EROI) and don't occupy too much land, in particular photovoltaics and wind power. It also includes infrastructure and industrial technologies that tend to recover resources and avoid the use of rare and disappearing mineral resources. The concept of 'efficiency' can also be included, with the caveat that it must not perpetuate dependency on fossil fuels (an example of such an ineffective strategy is moving from coal to natural gas).

So, how do we implement the sower's strategy? It may not need formal measures; we can see it as a form wisdom that already exists in people's minds and that leads to supporting investments in renewables in general. But we can also think of an international protocol (The Sower's Protocol) mandating that a fraction of the revenues obtained by fossil fuels must be dedicated to the development of a sustainable economy; in particular renewable sources. Revenues from a carbon tax could fund the protocol but, perhaps better, it could be directly applied to private or state owned energy companies. After all, investing in energy production is their job and we are not asking them to *pay* money, we are asking them to *make* money; albeit on a longer time scale. The protocol could also mandate non-monetary measures, such as for governments to ease permits and reduce bureaucracy for investments in sustainability.

No matter how it is implemented, the sower's strategy implies that we need to invest enough to create a new energy system before depletion (or global warming) makes it impossible to do so, but not so much that it would be an excessive burden on people's current welfare. It is a window of opportunity that will not be there forever, but which probably still exists today. Consider that the 58 largest world's oil and gas companies together had almost $6 trillion dollars in 2012 revenues (Wikipedia). If they were to re-invest just 4% of those revenues in renewable energy, that would double the amount spent today in the sector.

Irrespective of the actual fraction to be set apart, we can say that the sower's strategy, especially if implemented as a formal protocol, could be a true game changer in sustainability since:

1. It speeds up the transition, ensuring that sustainability and renewable energy will remain consistently supported.
2. It diverts investments from fossil fuels, forcing them to decline faster than they would if left to market forces alone. That speeds up the transition and eases the problem of global warming.
3. It stimulates the economy and creates jobs. It has the force of a positive approach: we are not asking people to stay home in the dark; we are asking them to work for the transition and make money from it!
4. The well-known principle of 'do not eat your seed corn' is something that everyone can understand. It will be hard for negative propaganda to distort it so much to make it appear as part of a Communist plot to enslave mankind (but never underestimate the power of PR tied to vested interests).

The sower's strategy by itself, formally or informally implemented, does not guarantee a smooth transition to a sustainable (and cool enough) world. It can't go against the laws of physics and it can't allow humankind to continue growing forever. Adapting our economy to renewable energy requires new infrastructure, rethinking industrial processes, adapting to the gradual reduction in the availability of all mineral resources. Among other things, we'll need to learn how to use renewable energy to power agriculture, to replace rare minerals with common ones (e.g. copper with aluminium), to manage waste as a resource and not as a burden, and much more.

Clearly, building up a completely sustainable economy is a difficult task, but it is not an impossible one. The only impossible thing is to keep civilization alive without energy and resources. The sower's strategy may give us a chance for the revolutionary transition.

Every year, our farmer ancestors faced a choice: how much of their harvest to keep as seeds? Save too much, and they would starve that year; save too little and they would starve next year. But they must have been making the right choices because they survived and we are their descendants. Today, we can learn from our ancestors how to make the right choices with fossil fuels too: save enough energy now to have enough energy in the future and also avoid disastrous climate change. Who hath ears to hear, let them hear.

Ugo Bardi (Italian, born 1952) is a professor in Physical Chemistry at the University of Florence. Prof. Bardi is a researcher on materials for new energy sources, a contributor for *The Oil Drum*. He is the president of ASPO Italy, a member of the scientific committee of the Association for the Study of Peak Oil and Gas (ASPO) and author of several books, including "The Limits to Growth Revisited".

2052 for Prospectors

Catherine Cameron

Jorgen Randers' book, *2052*, was written by and for 'Pioneers'. This group of people are inner directed and care very much about the future of the planet, the world we are leaving for our children, the risks we are running with pollution, our overuse of resources and the mismanagement of our planet. They make up some 38% of the UK population; more in Scandinavia.

A second group are outer directed 'Prospectors'. They make up 32% of the UK population. They are the biggest group in the USA. China and India are moving towards having Prospectors as the predominant group. They are interested in the right answer, being better and best, having a good time and displaying their success. It is thus critical that any messages about the future and what we can do to make it sustainable are framed in language that this group can respond to.

The third group are 'Settlers'. They represent around 30% of the UK population and are security driven. They will adopt behaviours once they are perceived as 'normal', i.e. when both Pioneers and Prospectors are doing it. Innovation and change comes from Pioneers, is then adopted by Prospectors and finally taken up by Settlers.

There are already a number of organisations that have used this approach to tailor their messaging to these different values-based groups, including Audi, Arsenal, BBC, Bass, CISCO, the Environment

Agency, Greenpeace, Haagen Daaz, the Henley Centre, Natural England, National Trust, Nestle, RSPB, Skoda, Shell, Unilever and Whitbread.

One proposed action is to rethink and reformulate the way in which the messages of 2052 – and the other Big Ideas by contributing Glimpse authors – are communicated, including in summary articles and public presentations.

Useful resources include *What Makes People Tick: The Three Hidden Worlds of Settlers, Prospectors and Pioneers*, by Chris Rose and the websites: www.cultdyn.co.uk and www.campaignstrategy.org.

Catherine Cameron (British and Guyanese, born 1963) was a member of the core team behind The Stern Review: The Economics of Climate Change. She is now director of Agulhas: Applied Knowledge, helping companies and organizations respond to the additional challenges to sustainability posed by climate change. She is a visiting fellow at the Smith School of Environment & Enterprise at the University of Oxford.

http://agulhas.co.uk/catherine_cameron.html

The Gaia Prize For Fertile Failures

John Elkington

Let's develop a global prize for fascinating failures in the field of sustainable business, markets and governance – encouraging faster sharing of what is working and, even more interestingly, what isn't and why. And also encouraging stretch ambitions, experimentation and outcomes. But it is worth recalling that if sustainability transition requires massive experimentation, the inevitable consequence will be a massive increase in the failure rate. None of us like to fail or to lose our jobs or investments, so let's help move the needle toward long-term success by celebrating and learning from the inevitable fascinating, fertile failures.

This is an embryonic idea that surfaced during the course of the 2052 Glimpse Authors session in Cambridge, during 2013. In a way, it could be a counterpart to Peter Diamandis's X Prize platform, catching at least some breakthrough innovators as they fall – and encouraging them to get back up on their feet and try again. In the same way that Icarus blazed the trail for aviators, so today's sustainability pioneers are pathfinders for new forms of value creation and politics. Their successes will help drive the sustainability transition, no question, but so too may the lessons flowing from at least some of their failures.

The purpose of the Gaia Prize for fertile Failures would be to short-circuit the processes of innovation, massively accelerating the evolutionary processes that have taken life from slime toward the stars in 3.8 billion years. This embryonic idea may well wither on the vine, but if there is interest in incubating and developing it, my email address is john@volans.com.

John Elkington (British, born 1949) is cofounder of Environmental Data Services (ENDS, 1978), SustainAbility (1987), and Volans (2008), where he is executive chairman. He has written seventeen books, sits on over twenty boards or advisory boards, and blogs at www.johnelkington.com/journal.

Rising Individualism Among the Young: A Great Challenge for Environmental Policy

Per Arild Garnåsjordet and Iulie Aslaksen

The large environmental problems of climate change and loss of nature – and their roots in overconsumption of natural resources - call for revitalization of collective political action. Yet individualism seems to be rising in the rich world, especially among the young. Although many young people support good causes, there is lack of engagement in collective political action. Conservative winds sweep across society and undermine the understanding of collective approaches to environmental policy.

Climate change and other systemic environmental problems are too large for individual solutions alone; they require collective approaches. It is difficult for the individual in our short life span to grasp the future consequences of the emerging trends of climate change and loss of nature. Overconsumption of resources threatens sustainability and calls for a change in public and private values to support a new ecological mindset. Yet the younger generation seems to be becoming more individualistic and less inclined to engage in collective political decisions. The issue is not lack of ethics or moral values. Many young people support good causes, do-good initiatives, and actively take part in political demonstrations.

However, they are caught up in the new dominant liberal and conservative notions of promoting individual rights and self-interest – disconnected from a notion of society and community as the basis for individual freedom. Life is a profoundly individualistic project. However, in terms of Maslow´s hierarchy of needs, freedom through self-actualization is always rooted in the fulfilment of basic needs and a sense of belonging within a community. Hence, society has to create and share freedom that supports self-actualization. By contrast, neo-liberal politics promotes an individual freedom disconnected from its roots in community – a kind of 'blue freedom'. This is not a useful compass for collective solutions to our looming environmental crises. What we need is social-democratic politics, which promotes an individual freedom grounded in community and solidarity with present and future generations – what we might call a 'red freedom'.

For decades, blue and the red approaches to freedom have enhanced and balanced each other. But now the scales may be tipping. Neo-liberal trends bring the ruthlessness of the competitive economy into education, health and the workplace. Environmental policies yield to private profit. Liberal parties have managed to brand freedom as their trademark – grasping the power of definition and equating freedom with liberalism. But the liberal freedom – selfishness disguised in blue velvet – as expressed by Norwegian public health professor Per Fugelli - can be a short-sighted version of self-interest which undermines the common good and a sustainable future.

Rising individualism makes it more difficult to find collective solutions to the climate crisis. Public benefits and support of the common good have been sacrificed for private goods. In the financial crisis, banks are saved while unemployment is rising. Natural resources, from fish stocks to hydropower, are privatized. Globalization threatens small-scale agriculture, with a loss of cultural landscape and identity. While private wealth and consumption increase, it has been followed by widespread denial of the environmental crisis. Public funds have been directed to support private wealth rather than to ambitious environmental policies. New institutions, beyond the attempts to find market solutions, quota systems and payment schemes, are called for to protect natural resources from overexploitation.

The social-democratic values from the labour movement and trade unions have been the great liberating forces of the 20th century. Freedom is the lost diamond of social-democracy – it is there and will always be there – but the everyday demands of government management have not allowed the diamond to shine in debate and rhetoric. The neoliberal political winds change the notion of freedom from individuals-in-community to individuals-in-selfishness. Is this what we want as a role model for the younger generation? The consequence of rising individualism is that only a limited group of young people is aiming to develop a complete political opinion, defining policy in term of collective political change.

The social democratic parties have paved the way to liberate people from poverty, lack of education and restrictive gender roles, creating freedom for individuals in society. These rights are not won once and for all; they need to be won by every new generation. We need to convey to the young generation that the political, social and economic rights we take for granted today are a result of long political struggle. Now the time has come to extend the power of collective action to a new approach to our environmental problems. The core issue is how we can encourage the young generation to organize and search for collective action in order to solve the environmental crisis. A promising attempt is the [group monitoring parliament members in Norway](#) to see if they keep their election promises.

We recommend encouraging young people to take part in political action, supporting environmental youth organizations, such as Young Friends of the Earth, and promoting climate change activism as a new path to collective political action, such as through 350.org and iMatter: Kids vs. Global Warming.

Per Arild Garnåsjordet (Norwegian, born 1945) is a geographer and senior researcher at Statistics Norway. From 1995–2006 he was managing director for Asplan Viak, a major consulting fim in urban and regional planning.

Iulie Aslaksen is senior researcher in the research department of Statistics Norway and works with sustainability indicators, the Nature Index, and policy for sustainable development.

Massive Mind-shifting for Sustainability

Thomas N. Gladwin

My 'big idea' is to induce a large scale, bottom-up and global movement to rapidly and powerfully instill sustainable cognition and perception into the minds of the future business, government and civil society leaders who will be taking over in the 2030s –

largely by radically transforming the form and content of education to emphasize novel thinking capacities.

The idea is not new. Robert Ornstein and Paul Ehrlich issued a clarion call over two decades ago for a process of conscious educated cultural evolution to change the way we think to save the human future. Massive mind-shifting is needed to overcome the profound biases against sustainability posed by:

1. Cognitively bounded 'biological minds' maladapted to the modern challenges of systemic complexity;
2. Obsolete 'worldview minds' guided by outmoded assumptions about how the world works;
3. Addicted 'contemporary minds' powerfully programmed to believe in myths and ideological doctrines that serve the interests of the few at the expense of the many; and
4. Delusional 'psychodynamic minds' that deploy ego-defense mechanisms to ward off any realistic and moral anxieties posed by awareness of ecological and social deterioration (see Gladwin. et. al. 1997 for an extensive review).

Back in 1992, in their book *Beyond the Limits*, Jorgen Randers and his colleagues wrote: 'how to bring into being a sustainable world that is not only functional but desirable is a question about leadership and ethics and vision and courage. Those are properties not of technologies, markets, government, corporations, or computer models but of the human heart and soul' (p. 217).

The power of this proposition is largely dismissed as impotent in the *2052: A Global Forecast*. The emergence of wise leadership is deemed unlikely. The exponential increase in smarter and more connected people is seen as insufficient to significantly change dominant values and behaviours. With a few minor exceptions, the role of moral duties and obligations, spirituality, religion and norms of fairness are viewed as irrelevant in shaping the future, despite predictions of massive human suffering. Any fundamental paradigm shifting toward sustainability is generally postponed to after 2052 due to the assumed persistence of dysfunctional short-termism, materialism, democracy, capitalism and bad management.

Are we really trapped in such a dark fate in which leadership, ethics and the creation of super-intelligence via the merger of minds and machines[1] will do little to alter the fate of humanity and the rest of life over the next 40 years?

What if we could find a way to radically transform global educational systems (of course with the aid of progressive scientific, media and foundation organizations) to accomplish the following:

---

[1] See the bold futurist Ray Kurweil's predictions of the emergence of super-intelligence over the next few decades in his book *How to Create a Mind*, 2012.

- Shift cognitive and perceptual heuristics in graduates from mechanistic to holistic to better cope with the complexities of coupled human and natural systems;
- Shift from human-nature separation toward mental reconnection with, and emulation of, nature's time-tested patterns, strategies, systems and processes;
- Shift from ingrained short-termism to enhanced anticipatory competencies and future time perspectives in order to respond consciously to long-term trends;
- Shift thinking from conformity to novelty, inducing a radical surge of creativity, imagination and trans-disciplinarity to address the world's most vexing challenges and emergent scarcities;
- Shift minds away from optimization to resilience, from efficiency to redundancy, and from homogeneity to diversity to boost adaptive capacities in the face of rising extremities, surprises and systemic risks; and
- Shift from amoral to moral minds where leaders know right from wrong, operate with a strong sense of fairness, put civic virtue ahead of greed, and display compassion rather than disinterest?

This is obviously a utopian vision of new-minded human thinking and it is hard to envision how a radical top-down repurposing of global educational systems to bring it about could be accomplished. If it is to happen, it will most likely arise from a bottom-up, networked, collaborative and cascading movement of hundreds of thousands of courageous and engaged educators working to change curriculums for the benefit of a sustainable human future[2].

Let's assume that this organic educational revolution on behalf of sustainable thinking does succeed. Just imagine what millions of new-minded (systemic, nature-connected, forward looking, highly creative, very adaptive and morally grounded) millennial leaders might be able to accomplish, say starting in the 2030s, when they take over the reigns of directing the world's organizations.

Might they collectively, interactively and synergistically lead the transformation to a much safer, more just, more verdant and more enlightened world? Might they speed up the rate of technological and societal change, the emergence of systemic corporate social responsibility and sustainable finance, the taking of the Fifth Cultural Step, the modification of capitalism toward the common good, the shift to a regenerative and solar-based economy, and most profoundly, the transformation toward sustainable well-being arising from the health of whole systems as the dominant paradigm ... all of these positive visions offered up by various glimpse authors in *2052: A Global Forecast*?

Might the emergence of transformative sustainable leaders become a significant 'trend breaker' in the 2030s, helping humanity mend its ways faster than the 2052 forecast predicts? Should it at least be considered a 'wild-card' that could make a huge difference if it does occur, albeit not easily captured in numbers and spreadsheets?

---

[2] For one small contribution, please contact me on tgladwin@umich.edu to acquire the syllabus for my course on "Sustainable Thinking, Design and Leadership" offered at The University of Michigan

The sustainability literature variously labels these new-minded forerunners of thought, action and spirit as positive deviants, tempered radicals, market rebels, bioneers, zeronauts, unreasonable people, and so on[3]. How many of these new leaders, with these new frames of comprehension, will we need to fundamentally alter the dismal fate of humanity and the earth offered up in the 2052 forecast? We don't know, but the cultural anthropologist Margaret Mead once offered a note of hope by asserting that we should 'never doubt that a *small* group of thoughtful, committed citizens can change the world; indeed, it's the only thing that ever has.'

References

Kurzweil, Ray, How to Create a Mind (New York: Penguin Group, 2012).

Ornstein, Robert and Paul Ehrlich, New World New Mind: Changing the Way We Think to Save Our Future (London: Paladin, 1991).

Gladwin, Thomas N. and William E. Newburry, and Edward D. Reiskin, "Why is the Northern Elite Mind Biased Against Community, the Environment, and a Sustainable Future?" in Max H. Bazerman, et. al., eds., Environment, Ethics and Behavior (San Francisco: New Lexington Press, 1997).

Meadows, Donella H and Dennis L. Meadows and Jorgen Randers, Beyond the Limits: Confronting Global Collapse, Envisioning a Sustainable Future (Post Mills, Vermont: Chelsea Green Publishing, 1992).

---

[3] The best work on the emergence of this new breed of leaders has been done by John Elkington, co-founder of SustainAbility and currently the Executive Chairman of Volans, a future-focused business working at the intersection of the sustainability, entrepreneurship and innovation movements.

Thomas N. Gladwin (American, born 1948) is the Max McGraw Professor of Sustainable Enterprise and associate director of the Erb Institute for Global Sustainable Enterprise at the University of Michigan. His teaching, research, and consulting focus on system dynamics, global change, and sustainable business.

Free Will is Highly Overrated

Ulrich Golüke

Jorgen wrote, in one of the last lines of the *2052* book, 'please help me make this forecast wrong.' And in one of his talks I saw on YouTube he said that one of his key assumptions was that values and preferences of people will not change (over his forecasting horizon).

But what if they do? This short article looks at why they might.

The end point of my argument is a little bit like Dag Andersen's in his glimpse – The fifth culture – but I develop my argument from a different starting point – and I argue that there is an inevitability to this – thus, hopefully, strengthening Dag's argument. It goes like this.

We humans need overarching stories – also known as paradigms – that help us make sense of our lives. These stories spell out the ideal, they name key actors, they specify the language, they determine the behaviour and they need to be clear about the energy powering the paradigm.

We currently live at the end of the 4th big story, namely the economic metanarrative. Its ideal is growth, actors are consumers and producers (note: not normal human beings!), its language is images and numbers, its defining behaviour is maximizing advantage and its fuel is fossil. Fossil fuel is the underbelly of the fading age of economics – one that allowed an ideology to take hold of never-ending growth and maximizing advantage.

Table 1: Historical Paradigms

	Heroic	Religious	Scientific	Economic
Ideal	Excellence	Goodness	Truth	Growth
Actors	Heroes & adversaries	Saints & prophets	Philosophers & scientists	Consumers & producers
Language	Stories	Scriptures & prayers	Logic & mathematics	Images & numbers
Behaviour	Competition	Obedience	Reason	Maximizing advantage
Energy	Solar	Solar	Solar	Fossil

Source: Adapted from Betty Sue Flowers

I've told you nothing new so far because you and I live it every day; it's in our bones and for most of us it is not a story, it is the *truth*. Still, this story is only the last in a series of sense-making stories, after the heroic, the religious and the scientific ones.

We need to ask ourselves why stories or paradigms shift? It is because the sense-making power of the old one fades away. The dissonances between the paradigm and reality accumulate, then cause pain and finally become unbearable. At that point a new story emerges. Inevitably so.

Since the economic story is no longer fit for purpose, what could the new, emerging paradigm look like? First, and foremost, it is regenerative. Just like after any life threatening illness, or any major disaster, we will concentrate intensely and relentlessly on getting back to heath: individually, collectively and environmentally. The new story's ideal is most like to be resilience. And resilience, I want to stress, *not* in any mysterious way[4], but really a rather simple

---

[4] I recently saw a book in Germany called *Resilience* and subtitled, freely translated, 'the mysterious inner strength that lets you succeed'.

structure of a capacity to cope: something that you can understand, develop, measure, use – even pass on when you die.

So far we've taken the resilience of the systems that support us for granted, because largely they were limitless. But thanks to 200 years of relentlessly 'taking costs out', we've ground them down so far that now we need to nurture them back to health. Just as we learn geology the day after the earthquake, we will learn about resilience the day after it's just about gone.

The language of the new story will be feedback (system dynamics) stories (scenarios), its dominant behaviour will be service and the key actors will be learner-builders. Finally, the new paradigm's fuel will be solar. And one of the consequences of a solar-fuelled paradigm is decentralization in all of its splendour and dullness.

Table 2: The Next Paradigm

	Regenerative
Ideal	Resilience
Actors	Learner-builders
Language	Feedback-stories
Behaviour	Service
Energy	Solar

All this is inevitable – trust me, free will is highly overrated. Two points to end with. First, let me remind you that despite the title of this little speech, fate only favours the prepared mind. So go off and prepare yourselves. Second, if you recall the transition from the scientific to the economic story, it becomes clear that despite the title of my article, the task ahead is daunting, to say the least. So go off and prepare!

Ulrich Golüke (born 1952 in Germany) studied systems dynamics with Dennis Meadows and has worked extensively with systems, scenarios and sustainability. In the 90ties he built up and ran the Scenario Unit of the World Business Council for Sustainable Development. For the last 12 years he has worked as a freelancer with Fortune 100 companies, universities, foundations and students. http://www.blue-way.net

Scorecard of Organisational Un-sustainability

Rob Gray

Although massively impractical at the moment, we must hold organisations to account for their influences on un-sustainability *and* remove warranty from the business community's capture of the sustainability agenda, their influence on the political sustainability agenda and their specious claims to sustainability (and/or journeys thereto).

I envisage that all large organisations would be ranked by something which genuinely sought to examine their environmental and social un-sustainability, i.e. unlike measures like the Dow Jones Sustainability Index. A traffic light system would be nice, but almost everybody would be red and there are only so many shades of red, so we might have to use minus scores.

Of course the idea is ridiculous because virtually no organisation produces the data necessary for us to assess it. For that, there needs to be a concerted effort to require all large organisations to discharge their social, environmental and sustainability accountability and desist from the present misleading (if well-intentioned) greenwash.

The components might well be cumbersome but would probably comprise:

1. A proper triple bottom line, based on a combination of a full stakeholder mapping and eco-balance reporting;
2. An ecological footprint; and
3. Some estimation of the (negative) impact on social justice.

Corporations are essential components of (un)sustainability and their accountability is crucial. The influence of large corporations is not in question: the largest companies are bigger than many national governments; multinational corporations dominate consumption, production and innovation throughout (especially) the developed world; they account for the bulk of world trade. More subtly, large corporations have a crucial influence on the global political economy, whether through their influence on governments, on attitudes, on information or on global decisions. So whether we are talking about consumption, pollution, waste, technical change, production, marketing, wealth and its distribution, affluence, wealth or choice, the role of the corporations is critical. We certainly cannot, therefore, discuss sustainability without discussing large corporations.

But just as it would be unhelpful to assume that all corporations undertake their roles in a manner completely malign to society and the planet, it would be foolish to assume that all corporate actions are benign and, indeed, contribute positively to all stakeholders. Societies need to be able to assess the balance between the malign and the benign consequences of corporate action. The making of such assessments is a cornerstone of democracy and it requires formal systems of accountability

It comes as no surprise that no organisation (of which I am aware) has come close to producing anything like this – despite all the self-adulatory propaganda. But individual organisations have produced the components of this to varying degrees: Traidcraft and CFS, Danish Steel Works, BFF. Nobody (as far as I know) has tried to address the social justice component.

In future, we must refuse to tolerate the specious use of the term "sustainability" with respect to organisational reporting without some explicit link to, say, 'limits to growth' data. We must demand organisational accountability as a duty not a voluntary matter of choice, explain and reiterate the practicability of a formal accountability and challenge business claims in this direction.

Rob Gray (British, born 1948) is a qualified chartered accountant and was editor of Social and Environmental Accounting Journal from 1991 to 2007. He is the author/co-author of over 300 books, monographs, chapters and articles. His books include *Accounting for the Environment* and *Accountability: Changes and challenges in corporate social and environmental reporting*. His work has appeared in nine languages other than English. He was Director of the Centre for Social and Environmental Accounting Research (CSEAR) from its inception in 1991 to 2012.

EC Legislation to Regulate Financial Indexes

Philippe Zaouati and Carlos Joly[5]

This note concerns the draft legislation proposed by the European Commission to help restore confidence in the integrity of financial benchmarks[6]. The European Commission wishes to extend its regulatory reach beyond LIBOR-setting to 'benchmarks that measure the performance of an investment fund'. The ultimate objective is to ensure the integrity of benchmarks by guaranteeing that they are not subject to conflicts of interest, *that they reflect the economic reality they are intended to measure* and are used appropriately' (emphasis added).

Four critical and important points concerning stock and bond market, and soft commodity benchmark indexes, should be brought to the European Commission's attention:

1. The most widely used benchmarks for equity and bond funds do not measure the economic reality they are intended to measure. Equity benchmarks generally reflect the relative size of the capital of companies as valued by the stock market, not their real

---

[5] Written in the following capacity: Philippe Zaouati, Chair, Cambridge Investment Leaders Group; Carlos Joly, Fellow, University of Cambridge Programme for Sustainability Leadership.
[6] Press Release of 18.09.2013; Proposal for a Regulation of the European Parliament and of the Council on indices used as benchmarks in financial instruments and financial contracts; Commission Staff Working Document Impact Assessment; and speech by Michel Barnier, De nouvelles mesures pour restaurer la confiance dans les indices de référence, à la suite des scandales du Libor et de l'Euribor.

economic value, and particularly when environmental and social externalities are taken into account. The stock markets are often notoriously wrong in pricing the real economic value of companies, as they establish prices that are either too high or too low in economic terms. Bond indexes may also be subject to the same errors, particularly sovereign bond indexes that reflect sovereign bond prices that may have little to do with political and economic fundamentals.

2. The prevalence of passive investment strategies in institutional investment (i.e. investment funds that seek to replicate the performance of a given stock or bond index or that are managed to a narrow tracking error relative to such an index) has the effect of exacerbating mispricing. Passive and near-passive strategies mean that the prices of underlying instruments (stocks or bonds) are automatically inflated or deflated according to how much money is placed to follow an index, further distancing the prices of the underlying instruments and the indexes from economic reality. This systematic fault can lead to systemic failure, creating bubbles and crashes in the stock and bond markets that have a negative effect on the economy.

3. As regards the EU's desire to promote long-term investment, and particularly long-term investment that supports the transition to a low carbon and greener economy, the most widely used stock market benchmarks are biased in favour of the past, in favour of companies that owe their success to economic and regulatory conditions that are unhelpful in the new economic context. Stock market capitalization is a poor criterion for future economic success and a particularly poor criterion for sustainable economic, environmental and social success. However, the way indexes are currently constructed, combined with the pernicious

effect of passive and near-passive investment, acts as a barrier to the progress of sustainable development. Capital is channelled disproportionately into old-economy companies rather than green economy companies, and companies that may wish to move strategically in line with sustainable development find little incentive from stock and bond markets to do so.

Benchmarks should appropriately measure and stimulate the transition to a low carbon economy by tilting capital towards the most responsible, innovative and efficient companies, better reflecting the moving economic present as opposed to reflecting – and through the transmission effect of passive investment strategies, exacerbating – the economically negative effects of valuation methods anchored in of the past.

4. Financial benchmark indexes for soft commodities (i.e. agricultural products) arguably promote financial behaviours that increase food prices and volatility. Ways can be found to limit the inappropriate financial use of such benchmarks, and for developing benchmarks that are more responsive to sustainable food production.

In sum, the most commonly used stock and bond market benchmark indexes cause economic harm, distort pricing information, and cause financial behaviours that are inimical with the EU's aspirations for a competitive low carbon economy. In short they constitute a barrier to the EU's economic, environmental and social welfare goals.

As the European Commission moves to regulate financial benchmarks, the responsible investment community will encourage it to consider the construction and wide adoption of stock and bond market benchmark indexes that are properly aligned with the low carbon and social goals to which the EU is committed.

As a partial and swift solution to this challenge, the Cambridge Investment Leaders Group could potentially offer its expertise to the European Commission in the possible development of guidelines for stock and bond market benchmarks that are more responsive to today's economic reality, and particularly to the reality of transitioning to a low carbon and more efficient economy.

If such guidelines are formulated and adopted, the ILG could make itself available for consultations with index providers for the construction of such indexes.

As leading investment institutions with significant market power, members of the ILG could potentially pilot test such indexes in their investment practice, and research their effects on investment risk, returns and impact on sustainable development.

Philippe Zaouati (French, born 1966) began his career in 1990 as analyst at Dresdner Group in Paris. He is supervising MIROVA, the newly created entity of Natixis dedicated to Responsible Investments. He is also chairing the Responsible Investment Working Group of the European Asset Managers Association (EFAMA). Philippe has written several books, including *Responsible Investing: in search of new values to finance.*

Carlos Joly (Argentinian, born 1947) has lived and worked in Europe for twenty-five years. He is an investment manager who over the years has pioneered various approaches to integrating environmental issues in portfolio management. He is currently chair of the Climate Change Scientific Avisory Committee of Natixis Asset Management in France.

Gone Surfing

Alan Knight

Should we work or go surfing? One grows the economy, but the other keeps you fit, helps you enjoy the best of the natural environment and is just good fun which is, after-all, what life is about. A sustainable future will find the optimum balance between economic growth, environmental growth and happiness. This builds on the concept of the triple bottom line by taking it to the heart of everyday lives. Economics will still be respected, but will be balanced with new, politically significant measurements for quality of life and the quality of the natural environment. Government policy will be geared not to success in one but the healthy balance of all three. Rather than economic growth the politics of the day will be environmental growth and personal growth with economics being the means to help deliver both.

Let's take an example. Cornwall is a remote region in the south west of England, rich in surfing beaches, countryside and spectacular coastlines. In 2013, however, its average wage was lower than the rest of England with productivity per working person also below average. The numbers were comparable with some of the emerging regions in Eastern Europe. Despite this, Cornwall scored well on quality of life, coming up as one of the regions in the England that people particularly enjoy living or visiting. In 2013, it was unknown in Cornwall whether this was a quirk of statistics or whether there was a deeper sophisticated link between the nature of peoples' work, their quality of life and their relationship with the natural environment. In a future sustainable world that relationship would be better understood and form the political agenda.

In 2013, the UK's prime national policy objective (like most countries in the world) was economic growth. At one level this is reasonable, but what is missing is the appetite to understand the cause, significance and long-term value of life satisfaction and the natural environment. Success is measured against economic outcomes, with growth being the key prize to chase. While prosperity matters, the missed opportunity for every economy is to understand more profoundly the relationship between that prosperity and peoples' happiness, wellbeing and the natural environment.

In a sustainable future, society will understand and manage the relationship between happiness, economic and the natural environment. All three will matter and be measured equally and policy will overtly seek to find the optimum balance between all three.

In 2013, there were not many examples of this kind of thinking; only anecdotes and emerging research. For example, in Cornwall it is not rare for even the most senior manager, when seeing perfect surf on their local beach, to end their working day a bit earlier and go surfing. Having travelled all day to view a house in Cornwall, the author of this report arrived at the estate office to see a note on the office door "gone surfing – back at 4pm". Welcome to Cornwall or welcome to a sustainable future? Is this good or bad economics? Surfing brings into Cornwall at least £64 million, with some organisations like Surfers Against Sewage arguing that it is much more. Environmental growth and personal growth could be achieved doubling this business.

Growing4life, a study by Thrive and Mind, demonstrates that a low cost but effective therapy for people suffering from mild to severe mental conditions was to provide supervised work in the natural environment, ranging from faming to horticulture. The therapy was more effective and at a much lower cost to all. Similarly, Growing Health Project, run by Garden Organic, sees the link between wellbeing and gardening, while the UK National Trust points out the benefits to children's health through their National Childhood Enquiry.

Tim Jackson, in his book *Prosperity without Growth*, argues that the continued pursuit of economic growth is locking us into unsustainability. However, so far there has not been a serious, policy changing debate on this. On the contrary, the need to tackle the national deficit and restore the economy is in danger of re-enforcing a growth centric policy.

We need to create safe spaces to talk about these issues – debates and workshops that draw together a quality of life index and agree measurements on the quality of the natural environment. We need new governance systems to better manage the link between natural, social and economic capital. Perhaps we could work with cabinet offices and treasury to seek their engagement and support for such measures on quality of life and natural environment. And of course, we need more people to spend time outdoors – so go wlaking, cycling or if you are lucky - go surfing!

Some useful websites on the subject include: www.thrive.org.uk, www.growinghealth.info and www.nationaltrust.org.uk.

Alan Knight (British, born 1964) specializes in corporate sustainability and product-centric sustainability for big brands (e.g., Virgin, Kingfishe, B&Q, SABMiller) and public policy (in UK government think tanks on sustainability, eco-labeling, and consumption). See www.dralanknight.com.

MOOCs Bachelor in Sustainable Development

Erling Moxnes

Research shows that people have great difficulties understanding and controlling dynamic systems. Therefore, people may argue and vote for policies that are not consistent with own preferences for sustainable development. Massive open online courses (MOOCs) that inform and correct misperceptions have the potential to reach millions of people. Courses can be offered free of tuition. Such courses may be of particular importance for change agents that can make use of such courses in their daily work. The 'big idea' is to develop a full distance-learning Bachelor program in sustainable development.

When making decisions, decision-makers, including voters in elections, must rely on their intuition, knowledge, and deep convictions. Learning for improved decision-making requires two crucial conditions to be satisfied: there must be learning opportunities and learning must be effective.

In terms of the first condition, massive open online courses (MOOCs) are a new invention that opens up learning possibilities for people all over the world. No longer do students have to travel to elite universities to get the best available education; it can be available at any computer with web-connections. Since every person in the world does not have internet connections and is not prepared for courses in complex issues, MOOCs are first of all important as a mean to educate change agents; people that can transform advanced knowledge into practical solutions at local levels.

Addressing the second condition, learning about complex issues requires teaching methods that question existing understanding, help students develop intuition, foster analytical skills, and enable transfer and application of knowledge. Interactive, online teaching can be used for these purposes through the use of challenging tasks in the form of simulators, probing questions and suggested answers for gradual knowledge construction, simulation models to learn about structure and behaviour of systems, and application tasks where acquired knowledge is put to practical use. Each task can be followed by debriefing videos that explain the specifics and generalize the results.

Let's look at an example of how this may apply in practice. People tend to assume that the concentration of greenhouse gases in the atmosphere vary in pace with yearly emissions. Hence, people are inclined to opt for wait-and-see policies, where the growth in emissions is halted only when problematic climate change is observed. To challenge these incorrect assumptions, students get to see historical data from the early 1980s when the atmospheric concentration increased steadily in spite of stagnating emissions. To understand why halting emissions is not sufficient to stop the increase in the concentration, students work with simulation models and use these to explore policies for sustainable development.

An online, distance-learning course in Natural Resources Management (GEO-SD660) offered by the University of Bergen is a first course that meets the two above conditions. The example with greenhouse gases is from one of the cases in the course. After the pilot class in 2013, increasing numbers of students will get access to the course. The 'big idea' is to develop a full Bachelor program in sustainable development.

Erling Moxnes (Norwegian, born 1952) is a professor in system dynamics at the University of Bergen (Norway). He has a PhD from Dartmouth College (USA). He has published on resource management and economics with a focus on misperceptions of dynamics and on policy. http://www.uib.no/rg/dynamics

A Floor Tariff for Renewables in Least Developed Countries

Terje Osmundsen

I propose a risk sharing mechanism targeting enhanced bankability of solar and wind projects in Least Developed Countries (LDCs). The floor tariff would be applicable to renewable power projects with Power Purchase Agreements (PPAs), but without a fixed, guaranteed tariff for the PPA period.

Renewable energy developers in LDCs with projects that have more than a 10-year payback period should be eligible for a minimum sales price guarantee. The guaranteed minimum sales price – the floor tariff – could be indexed to the country's official average wholesale tariff for electricity.

Many more solar and wind projects could be built, if the project finance could include a possible third-party guarantee against a possible – but highly unlikely – fall in the relevant market prices for energy during the 20 year period. If such a mechanism was available, Power Purchase Agreements could become bankable even in cases where off-takers – often government-owned utilities in poor financial health – are unable or unwilling to commit to a fixed tariff for the whole 20-year contract period.

The guarantee could be issued by a pool of industrialised countries as a precursor the announced new UN-initiated Green Fund and could be managed by the International Finance Corporation (IFC) or one of the other multilateral development banks active in

LDCs. Should the guarantee be drawn upon to cover a material loss on specific contracts, the loss should be counted for as development aid by the donor countries. Alternatively, it could be covered by proceeds from the Green Fund established as part of a new global Climate Treaty.

One of the conditions for issuing the guarantee should be that the alternative to the project is increased consumption of fossil fuels. In addition, the guarantee should in any case only say 80% of a potential loss due to unforeseen fall in the contract's reference price, with the remaining 20% to be covered by the developer.

Why is this is an important idea? Utilities and large companies in Africa and parts of Asia and Latin America continue to rely on expensive and polluting diesel and heavy fuel oil to meet the rapidly growing demand for electricity. This happens despite the fact that a substantial share of the demand could be me met by solar or wind power, at a lower cost. In several countries in Africa, wind and solar is now cost-competitive not only against the incremental generation cost but even compared to the average generation costs in the country.

However, except for South Africa, only a handful of utility-scale solar or wind Independent Power Producers (IPP) have been financed and constructed in Sub-Saharan Africa, Latin America and South East Asia. The main hurdle is the challenge of reaching agreement with the off-takers on the key requirements of bankability, most often the take-or-pay commitment and the fixed tariff for the 20-year contract period. Given the high investment costs, such commitments are required to enable private sector financing of solar and wind projects.

However, some potential off-takers, including government-owned utilities are reluctant to sign 20-year Power Purchase Agreements with a locked-in tariff for the whole period. Reasons for this reluctance may vary, but very often it is motivated by a perception that market energy prices will fall in longer term. When discussing the issue with stakeholders, one typically hears statements like 'When the new hydro or gas-fired power plant is built, energy prices will fall', or "with equipment prices falling, it's better to wait', or "20 years is a very long time; so much can happen'.

There have been a few examples in Europe and the United States where developers have tried to finance utility-scale solar photovoltaic (PV) projects with revenues linked to the wholesale energy price index, but so far unsuccessfully I believe. However, there are examples where the proposed floor price could be applicable:

- In Ghana, where the government has announced a feed-in-tariff fixed for 10 years only. After the 10-year period, the tariff will be reviewed every 2 years, partly reflecting the wholesale energy index.
- In Senegal, where generation costs are high, but the government and utility company Senelec believe generation costs will fall and therefore hesitates to enter into 20 year fixed tariff contracts
- In Namibia, where the official plans are based on the realisation of a 800 MW gas fired power station in 2017, with short term investments in expensive oil-and diesel- powered generators instead of solar.

Terje Osmundsen (Norwegian, born 1957) is a former state secretary to the prime minister of Norway, with a varied career from international business (natural gas, engineering, telecom) to publishing and scenario-based consulting. Since 2009, he has been senior vice president of Scatec Solar AS, a leading developer and supplier of solar power plants.

http://energiogklima.no/nyhetsblogg/terje-osmundsen/

Collaboration Among Mediterranean Islands

Thymio Papayannis

The Mediterranean Basin has always been a tumultuous region of the world. At present, at the beginning of the third millennium, it is being subjected once more to severe stresses. European countries in the North – mainly Greece, Portugal and Spain– are facing financial collapse within the general malaise that threatens the Eurozone. In North Africa and the Middle East, political unrest, leading to armed conflict, is prevalent and hopes for a peaceful and democratic 'Arab Spring' have dissipated.

These economic and political stresses, combined with deep poverty in certain countries of Africa and Asia, have fuelled population movements from the South and East to the North, creating humanitarian and social problems, while tourist flows towards the Mediterranean are for the moment on the increase. Throughout the Basin, there is a growing mixing of populations and cultures, while traditional social and family structures are weakening. Demographic increases and unsustainable development pressures lead to coastal artificialisation and environmental degradation. The impacts of climate change are becoming visible, with desertification already clearly observed in Cyprus.

The Mediterranean is rich in islands with great diversity in size, natural resources and history. Two of them (Cyprus and Malta) are already states and members of the European Union. They are joined in size by Corsica, Crete, Euboea, Majorca, Rhodes, Sardinia and Sicily, with populations ranging from 100 thousand to 5 million, among which autonomy trends are growing. There are 12 other medium-size islands with populations of 30 000 to 100 000 (Lesbos, Chios, Zakynthos, Salamis, Kefallonia, Samos and Kos in Greece, Ischia and Elba in Italy, Gozo in Malta, Minorca in Spain and Djerba in Tunisia)[7], and various archipelagos with a multitude of small islands, some uninhabited.

Tourism and leisure are the major economic and social activities in the Mediterranean Islands and have had a serious impact in various sectors and at many levels. Resort housing, addressed to affluent Northern Europeans, but also wealthy Middle Easterners, has been increasing. This is being supplemented by small-scale, quality agriculture, as well as declining fisheries and increasing aquaculture. Industry exists in some of the larger islands, such as Sicily and Corsica. Transport and illegal immigration constitute key problems, along with the provision of satisfactory social and technical services, particularly to the smaller islands.

Contacts and commerce among the islands has been pronounced, especially under the great Empires (Macedonian, Roman, Byzantine, Ottoman), with various degrees of political unity. Conflict has been continuous and piracy has played a significant role[8]. In the modern world, national frontiers have fractured the Mediterranean and rendered contacts difficult. However, the benefits of joint actions to face challenges and to cultivate economic synergies are evident. Immigration and tourism are two areas in which inter-island communication might produce positive results. A creative mix of populations and cultures, carrying their particular heritage, skills and capacities, could magnify these.

---

[7] Data from Wikipedia (accessed on 11 September 2013).
[8] Norwich, J. J. (2010), *The Middle Sea*, London, the Folio Society.

GREAT IDEAS FOR CREATING A MUCH BETTER WORLD

A first step in furthering cooperation – focusing on specific sectors of common interest, such as tourism, public health and higher education – would be a loose organisation between Cyprus and Malta, perhaps in the framework of the Union for the Mediterranean, which could eventually evolve into a formal treaty. Other large islands could be encouraged to join this treaty, initially in an informal but substantial manner, while maintaining their national linkages. Gradually smaller islands would decide to join this cooperation network.

Architect Stefano Boeri and others have proposed the utopian idea of a 'Free Confederation of the Mediterranean Islands' a few years ago, focusing on the Aegean Sea[9]. A gradual process might have more chances of success, proceeding by small steps in various sectors and levels. It might take half a century before the Mediterranean Island Federation becomes a reality, but it is these first positive and promising steps that are important. They must be taken now.

Further information

Mediterranean Institute for Nature and Anthropos (Med-INA) at www.med-ina.org

---

Thymio Papayannis (Greek, born 1934) is an architect-planner. A graduate of MIT, he has been involved for the past thirty years in the conservation of natural and cultural heritage in the framework of the Ramsar Convention and its Mediterranean Wetlands Initiative

---

[9] Boeri, S. (2007), 'A Mediterranean Utopia: The Aegean City and the Birth of the Free Confederation of Mediterranean Islands', in *domus* issue 900 (pp 279-290).

(MedWet), WWF International, IUCN, and the Mount Athos Holy Community. He is president of the Society for the Protection of Prespa.

Compulsory Vacation: Reducing the Human Ecological Footprint Through More Annual Leave

Jorgen Randers

Many environmentalists worry about continuing growth in the rich world. More specifically, they worry about the continuing growth in the production of goods and services – because of the concomitant increase in the ecological footprint. They worry that growth in GDP will increase the amount of resources used – and the amount of pollution generated – beyond what the world can handle in a sustainable manner. Their dream is to reduce the 'ecological footprint' per person – ideally without lowering general wellbeing.

Most voters do not agree; they argue that continued growth is necessary and desirable for many reasons: to increase income, to avoid unemployment, and to fund pensions for the rising number of old. These objectives, they argue, are more important than lowering the ecological footprint. For the time being the pro-growth group carries the floor, even in the rich world.

But what if a rich nation, contrary to expectation, did decide to reduce its ecological footprint? Could it be done? I believe it could, and that the simplest method would be to increase the amount of annual vacation: adding several extra vacation days every year, for all citizens, and through legislation that requires people to take more time off. Let me explain.

The total annual production of a nation (GDP) can be seen as its number of workers multiplied with the output per worker per year.

The output per worker per year can be seen as the number of hours worked per year multiplied with his/her output per hour. So, by reducing the average number of hours worked per person per year, one can achieve a reduction in the GDP (relative to what it would otherwise have been) – and, ultimately, a reduction in the footprint. In summary: more vacation, less time at work, lower production, less footprint.

Would it really work? Yes, if voters really supported the idea. The simplest proof is that many rich countries did already systematically shorten the work year – with success. From 1970 to 2005, labor productivity in Norway increased by around 3 % per year on average. During the same period, incomes rose by around 2 % per year. The rest – about 1 % per year – was taken as increased leisure. The number of hours per year in a 'full time' job decreased from around 1,800 to 1,400 hours per year (see Figure appended). If Norwegians as an alternative had followed the US model, and kept hours long and annual leave at the traditional minimum, their annual incomes would have been 1.3 times higher than they are. But Norway chose differently, and Norwegians do not believe they would have been happier with more money and less leisure.

Similarly, labour unions in Denmark were once asked to choose between a) 3% increase in the annual wage for the ensuing year, and b) 0% increase in the annual wage, but 3% fewer workdays. They overwhelmingly voted for the latter. Rather than asking for more money, the Danes asked for more leisure. Which makes a lot of sense in a rich country (but does not make sense in a poor country where the prime need is for more production – goods and services). Notice that the wage *per hour worked* stayed the same in the Danish case.

Note that more 'compulsory vacation' might not lower the ecological footprint even if adopted as national legislation. Employers might choose to compensate for the reduction in hours worked per person by hiring more persons. This would work as long as there was a pool of unemployed to draw from. In this case more 'compulsory vacation' simply would distribute the available work among more people. More people would have a job, but on average working fewer hours per year. This would be good for employment, for distributional equity, and (probably) for wellbeing. But it would not have the intended effect of lowering the GDP and the ecological footprint.

Increasing the amount of 'compulsory vacation' is equivalent to reducing the maximum allowable hours of paid work per person per year. Thus another way to introduce more 'compulsory vacation' would be to pass legislation that limits the number of hours of paid work that anyone can have during a year. But this may be less realistic, since the voter may perceive a limit on the number of hours of paid work per year as an unwelcome restriction of freedom. The voter is more likely to accept legislation that provides more time off while maintaining his/her annual salary. I believe legislation that increases the number of vacation days has a fair chance of being passed in the rich world.

Longer annual leave means that more shifts will be needed to fill a 24/7 job – or in other words more irregular work patterns. But these are administrative problems that could be solved if one really wanted to increase the amount of leisure. And there could be control problems – people working even if they were supposed to be vacationing – in countries with imperfect systems for tracking worker income (normally for taxation purposes).

If the ambition were to keep the GDP constant, the length of the work year would have to be reduced at the same pace as the rate of productivity growth. And if the work force was growing, the work year would need to be cut even faster. A numerical example is useful. If productivity growth in the rich world stays around 1% per year, and population growth around the same, the length of the work year would have to be lowered by 2% per year to keep the GDP constant. This would amount to some 32 hours per year or 4 days of increased vacation every year. That is quite a bit!

If the GDP were held constant in real terms, the ecological footprint would most likely decline, due to continued technological advance (for example continued reduction in the use of energy and resources per unit of GDP). If the footprint were to be cut faster, one would simply increase the amount of 'compulsory vacation' given per year.

What would people do if they were forced to reduce the amount of paid work? What would people in the rich world do if they had to spend more time away from the office? I believe they would be doing all those things they currently dream about doing: more time with the family, more hobbies, more pleasure. And when the amount of leisure got even longer, they would start doing themselves what they currently pay other people to do: cooking food, maintaining their home, and providing care. And if this structural shift got so far as to generate unemployment in the restaurant, maintenance and care sectors, this could be handled by further increases in the amount of compulsory vacation. The limited amount of available (paid) work would be split evenly among the citizens. Instead of having some people unemployed, all would be having longer vacations.

I doubt that compulsory vacation will ever be introduced in order to reduce the ecological footprint. But the policy of more compulsory vacation might be adopted in the rich world for a completely different reason. Shortening the work year serves to split the available work among more workers. Hence compulsory vacation may be seen as the best solution to another problem that is going to bother the industrialized world over the next several decades: namely rising unemployment caused by slow GDP growth.

Figure 1: Hours of paid work per employee per year in US (top), Germany (middle) and Norway (bottom): 1970-2005

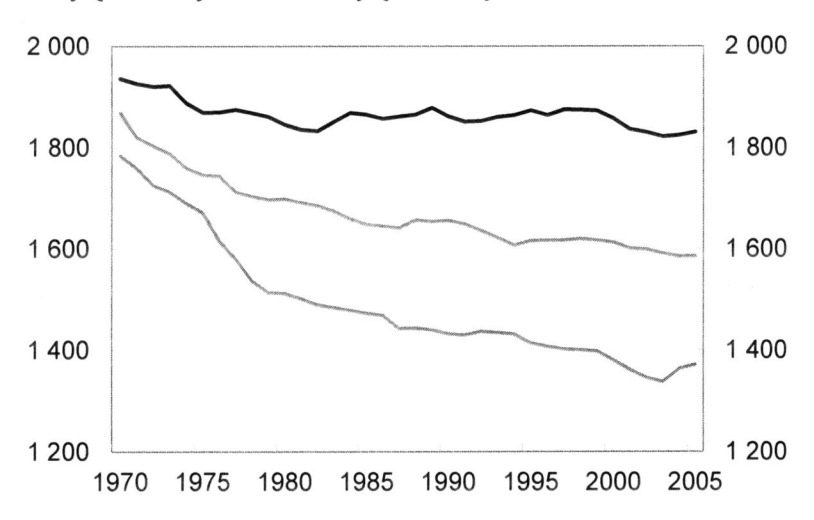

Source: OECD; via Norges Bank 2006

Jørgen Randers (Norwegian, born 1945) is Norwegian and a professor of climate strategy at BI Norwegian Business School. He has divided his long professional career evenly among the research,

NGO, and corporate worlds, always with a focus on sustainable development. He coauthored The Limits to Growth in 1972.

The 5-Year Global Sustainability Olympics: A Vision From the Future

Rasmus Reinvang

In his sober and harsh global forecast for the development of the world economy towards 2052, professor Jørgen Randers ends with a plea: 'Please help make my forecast wrong!' This idea-piece is an attempt to contribute to a global movement doing just that, by ensuring a more sustainable and equitable development on our planet.

The idea was triggered by a text written by the Czech writer-dissident and president Vaclav Havel, published in 1986 when then Czechoslovakia was still under Soviet-backed Communist one party rule. Possibly it reflects thoughts developed under his imprisonment during the period 1979-1983. The fact that it is quoted here is an example of the power and potential effect of cultural expressions – the exact power we would like to harness in the '5-Year Global Sustainability Olympics'.

At one point in Central Europe in the mid 1980s, the dissident sat down and wrote by hand, or maybe on one of those mechanic typewriters of yesteryear, with a cigarette burning in the ashtray beside him on the table (Havel was a heavy smoker):

'A change will have to derive from human existence, from the fundamental reconstitution of the position of people in the world, their relationship to themselves and to each other, and to the universe. If a better economic and political model is to be created,

then perhaps more than ever before it must derive from profound existential and moral changes in society.'[10]

Sustainable and equitable global development is not impossible today. It is not waiting for some new technology to be invented, developed and/or commercialized. It is simply a management challenge; a question of leveraging proper understanding, will and skills. Fundamentally, the world we create is an extension of our understanding of ourselves and the culture we create to express ourselves. So let's nourish a culture of sustainability. Here is how the vision might unfold.

In 2015 an idea spread across the globe: the idea that an increasingly globalized economy, coupled with increasing and global environmental challenges, has to be met by cultural approaches that enable fundamental change towards sustainability. In short, the world's populations need to leverage the elements of their unique cultural traditions that support sustainable ways of existing on this planet – and to discard traditions, incentive structures and practices enabling and promoting excessiveness and unsustainability.

At the UN General Assembly in 2015, a Commission was mandated to start and facilitate a global creative process to explore, document and celebrate how the world's different cultural and religious traditions in various ways meet the need for a 'culture of sustainability'. Using methodologies from the social sciences, the Commission defined 10 broad criteria of sustainability, based on universalism, which would have to be met.

The Commission coined the term 'Sustainability Memes', meaning a consistent set of ideas or cultural practises that embody a

---

[10] Vaclav Havel: Living in Truth, 1986.

sustainable way of operating in the world. A Sustainability Meme can be on different levels and of different types; for instance Buddhist ethics, the farmer's credo to pass the farm on in a better condition than it was when he/she received it, clever and fair policies for redistribution of wealth, or cultural traditions and expressions that nourish a deep understanding and feeling of connectedness and joint responsibilities.

The Commission also launched the concept of 'Sustainability Spectacles', stressing that sustainability needs to move from the technical and scientific to the cultural and emotional sphere. Sustainability Memes should be identified and celebrated in Sustainability Spectacles involving the general public, such as shows, exhibitions and competitions at all levels. Sustainability Memes should thereby be recognized and become a source of pride and identification, for a multi-faceted cultural sustainability revolution to roll out across the planet. Technologies enabling participation of the general public in this process should be employed.

Finally, the Commission challenged all the world's governments and social groups to identify, document and present selected Sustainability Memes at the first 'Global Sustainability Olympics' in 2020 – to be held every 5 years.

The Commission's framework triggered a spontaneous bottom-up process across the globe. In all countries, governments set out to document their country's unique contributions to a global culture of sustainability, as did religious organizations, professional communities and all kinds of organizations. In many areas competitions were launched where the public could vote for their favourites via mobile phones or the internet, first at national levels and then at regional levels, and for different professions even at global levels. This spurred a 'race to the top' in a wide array of fields and generated enthusiasm and new local, national and regional celebrities.

In 2017, the Commission presented the rules for the Global Sustainability Olympics in 2020. 100 disciplines of competition were identified, covering a wide array of fields, from ethics to public transportation systems and sustainable recreation practises. Each region had a certain number of spots, for which representatives from that region would compete in regional competitions. Within the framework of the Sustainability Criteria, each region was free to choose their winners according to local preference and argumentation.

The 2020 Global Sustainability Olympics was the first virtual and participatory global event, with the competitors being linked-up from their own countries and a global audience voting for their favourites via mobile phones or the Internet. In each category the participants would present their meme in a form of their own choice during five minutes. The three Sustainability Memes with the most votes in each category became Olympic Sustainability Ambassadors (OSAs). After being granted a 1 million dollar budget each, 300 OSAs toured the world, promoting their Sustainability Meme until the next Olympics.

The Global Sustainability Olympics spurred a positive, participatory and dynamic integration of the wonders of mankind's cultural traditions leading to 'profound existential and moral changes in [the global] society'. Of-course, identifying Sustainability Memes and creating Sustainability Spectacles can be done by anyone, anywhere – now.

Rasmus Reinvang (Danish, born 1970) is an indologist who has lived and worked in China. He has a PhD from the University of Oslo (Norway), has previously taught at Copenhagen University (Denmark) and the University of Gdansk (Poland), and has more than ten years' experience with nonprofit and consultancy work elated to sustainable development in an international context.

Finance 2050: Greening Financial Regulation

Nick Robins and Catherine Cameron

To date, most of the focus of sustainability policy has been on reforming the 'real economy': agriculture, cities, energy, transport, waste and water, etc. Financial policy has remained largely untouched – something that needs to change urgently if capital is to flow at scale and speed away from damaging and towards sustainable activities. Our 'big idea' is to mobilise the expertise of the 2052 glimpse authors to accelerate, inspire and converge embryonic initiatives to green financial markets: a Finance 2050 initiative.

Over the past two decades, the sustainable finance movement has achieved considerable progress in terms of making environmental, social and governance issues a strategic priority for mainstream institutions. From a regulatory perspective, the movement has achieved greatest impact in the limited field of corporate sustainability disclosure.

What has pushed forward these largely soft, voluntary initiatives have been successive financial crises – notably the equity bubble of the late 1990s and the credit crunch of the 2000s – which revealed the structural flaws in the prevailing financial system, notably volatility, short-termism, excess remuneration and criminality. As the financial community gears up for the dual 2015 deadlines on climate change and sustainable development, there is growing awareness that fresh efforts are required to confront these systemic issues.

For example, there are rising concerns that well-intentioned financial regulation – such as Basel 3 and Solvency 2 – could place unintended barriers in the way of low-carbon infrastructure. Equally, investors are increasingly aware of the risk of stranded assets that could flow from Carbon Tracker's 'unburnable carbon' analysis – and yet financial regulation provides no guidance on how institutions and markets can avoid or prevent capital destruction.

Currently a number of initiatives are beginning to touch on this agenda – notably Bloomberg's Finance for Resilience, the Global Commission on the Economy & Climate, preparatory work by UNEP FI on Ban-ki Moon's September 2014 Climate Summit, and Aviva's project for a 'capital raising plan' for sustainable development. But none of these have an exclusive focus on financial regulation – and none bring the longer-term systems perspective of 2052 and its Glimpse authors, including Carlos Joly's proposal to reform investment benchmarks.

We propose that we pull together a small group of 2052 Glimpse authors interested in financial regulation to develop proposals for 1-2 outcomes within the financial regulation arena, focusing on such areas as fiduciary duty, banking rules and benchmarks. We could also develop new 'prospector' messaging and produce a distinctive follow-up paper in 2014 as the first in a series of Finance 2050.

Some useful websites and resources include Finance for Resilience, EU Low-Carbon Investment and New Financial Sector Regulation, **and** Lenses and Clocks: Financial Stability and Systemic Risk.

Nick Robins (British, born 1963) is a sustainable investor and business historian. He has worked on the policy, business, and financial dimensions o sustainable development for the past twenty years and is author of The Corporation That Changed the World: How the East India Company Shaped the Modern Multinational and coeditor of Sustainable Investing: The Art of Long-Term Performance.

Catherine Cameron (British and Guyanese, born 1963) was a member of the core team behind The Stern Review: The Economics of Climate Change. She is now director of Agulhas: Applied Knowledge, helping companies and organizations respond to the additional challenges to sustainability posed by climate change. She is a visiting fellow at the Smith School of Environment & Enterprise at the University of Oxford.

Population Scenarios for 2052 and Beyond: Dramatic Decline?

Harald Siem

This contribution is seeking to alert readers to the fact that the global population size is very likely to shrink dramatically from 2052 onwards. Whereas population forecasts since the population conference in Bucharest 1974 have been scaled back from a leveling off at 14 billion to 8 billion, to be reached around 2050, most people are concerned with what they perceive as a population explosion that is to come. Little is said about the implosion after 2052, which is a very likely scenario.

In a recent article in Demographic Research, the global population size is modeled with alternative fertility rates (0.75 – 2.5) combined with maximum life expectancy of 90, 100 and 120 years. If global fertility in the long run converges to a level of 1.5 – which is slightly below the 2009 average level in the European Union of 1.59 – then, after peaking around the middle of the century, the world population would return to the current level of seven billion people by 2110. By the end of the 22nd century it would fall below three billion under the scenario of 100 years life expectancy in all parts of the world.

If, more dramatically, the global fertility rate approaches the figure currently seen in East Asia, below one, the population will be below four billion at the end of this century. The demographic transitions today happen fast, and the two-child norm is not necessarily the end-point of transition. Today already, sizeable populations exist where the voluntary chosen ideal family size is heavily concentrated around one child per woman, with total fertility rate as low as 0.6-0.8.

Figure 2: Global population scenarios: 2000-2300

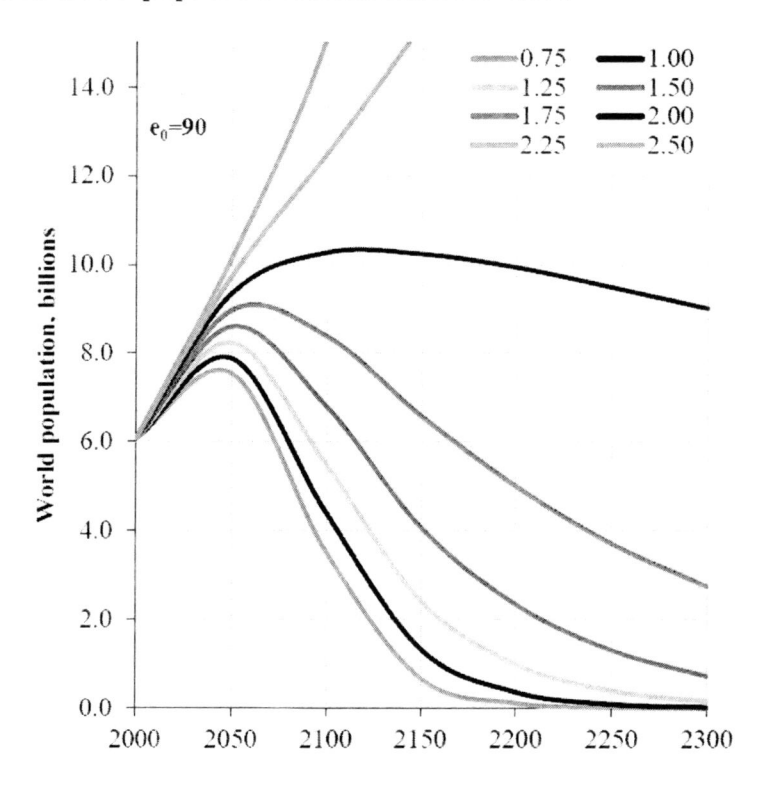

Source: Basten, Lutz and Scherbov: Very long range population scenarios to 2300 and the implication of sustained low fertility

Harald Siem (Norwegian, born 1941) is a medical doctor with a master's in public health, trained in Basel, Oxford, Oslo, and Harvard. He has worked as a district medical officer then atthe University of Oslo, and for the Oslo city health administration, International Organization for Migration, and WHO in Geneva, and now works in the Norwegian Directorate of Health.

Longer Life Products

Chris Tuppen

Extending warranties will encourage improved design for longevity and repair. This will reduce waste to landfill, reduce the use of increasingly scarce raw materials and reduce carbon emissions associated with mining, refining and manufacture.

We live in a throw away society. When products fail we more often than not go out and buy new ones. And when we throw the old products away, at worst they end up in landfill, and at best they will be fragmented with some of the materials being recycled. Many feel that a combination of pressure on companies to grow revenues and an in-built consumer preference for cheaper products has led to products designed to be cheap to manufacture rather than cheap to own over the long term.

In developed economies, it didn't used to be like this – one just needs to talk to a person that grew up in the middle of the last century. And in many developing economies they still recover every last bit of value out of products.

Figure 3: Bicycle repair shop in India

So what could be done to address this? One simple solution would be to extend product warranties. Recent consumer research[11] in the UK has shown that customers both expect and want product warranties to be longer than they often are, and that they are prepared to pay more for this.

---

[11] Evidence of consumer demand for retailer services on electrical products that offer alternatives to new product purchase, WRAP, 2013. http://www.wrap.org.uk/content/resource-efficient-business-models-consumer-research

Figure 4: Expected and wanted standard warranties for durable products

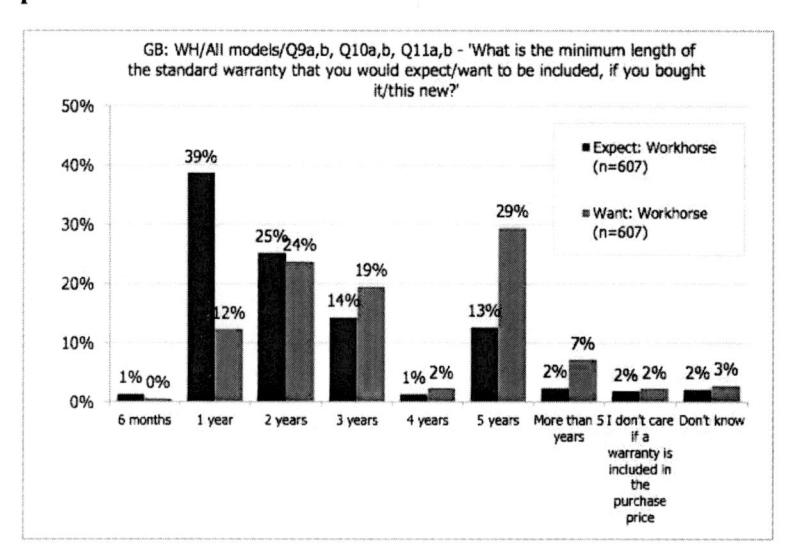

GB: WH/All models/Q9a,b, Q10a,b, Q11a,b - 'What is the minimum length of the standard warranty that you would expect/want to be included, if you bought it/this new?'

Duration	Expect: Workhorse (n=607)	Want: Workhorse (n=607)
6 months	1%	0%
1 year	39%	12%
2 years	25%	24%
3 years	14%	19%
4 years	1%	2%
5 years	13%	29%
More than 5 years	2%	7%
I don't care if a warranty is included in the purchase price	2%	2%
Don't know	2%	3%

Source: WRAP, 2013

Figure 5: Willingness to pay for longer standard warranties for durable products

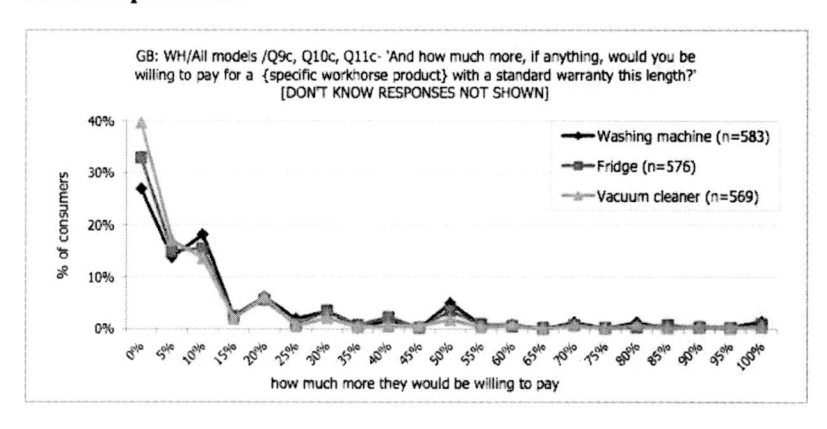

GB: WH/All models /Q9c, Q10c, Q11c- 'And how much more, if anything, would you be willing to pay for a {specific workhorse product} with a standard warranty this length?' [DON'T KNOW RESPONSES NOT SHOWN]

- Washing machine (n=583)
- Fridge (n=576)
- Vacuum cleaner (n=569)

x-axis: how much more they would be willing to pay (0% to 100%)
y-axis: % of consumers

Source: WRAP, 2013

Product reliability follows a classic 'bathtub' curve with high levels of infant mortality as manufacturing defects manifest themselves, followed by the serviceable life and finally the wear out phase. The manufacturer's or retailer's liability generally extends little beyond the warranty period[12], which is often no more than one year. If this was extended then the manufacturer would be encouraged to design for better reparability and longer life. A beneficial side effect would be to make end of life refurbishment and product reuse far more cost effective.

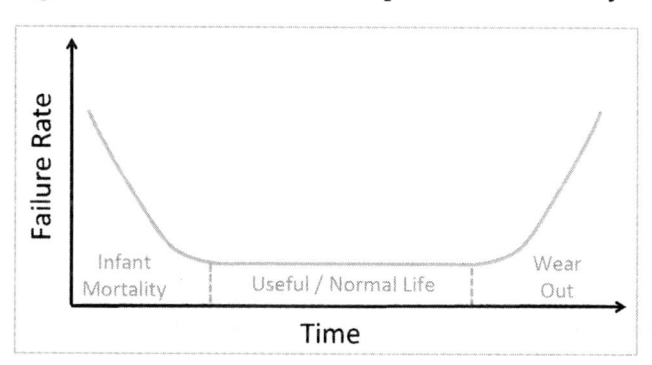

Figure 6: 'Bathtub' curve for product reliability

The bottom line of this from an environmental perspective is significant. A product that lasts twice as long results in a halving of the number of products entering the waste stream, a halving of manufacturing feedstock consumption and halving of the CO_2e emissions associated with raw material extraction, processing and manufacturing.

---

[12] This is not entirely accurate – at least for the UK. The law requires a product to be fit for purpose irrespective of the stated warranty period. However, it is a lot more difficult to claim against this legal provision than it is to claim against a standard warranty.

A good case study is ISE, a small washing machine supplier based in Kilmarnock, Scotland. Their machines are designed to be robust, reliable and repairable through a 'no parts mark up pledge' when the guarantee period runs out. In fact the company's stated objective is to reduce the amount of washing machines sold each year. On the surface, this is a very unusual approach for a business that depends on selling new products.

All ISE machines are made by Asko, based in Vara, Sweden in a factory that traditionally supplies commercial machines to the UK market. The machines are sold online and delivered and installed via a network of independent service engineers. Their standard model is designed to last at least 8,000 cycles and comes with a full ten year parts and labour warranty. Components are made from engineered metal rather than moulded plastic and the grades of steel used are of the highest. ISE say this makes them 4–6 times more durable than good quality domestic machines, and over 10 times more durable than 'value machines' sold by the major chains.

ISE encourage the longest possible life for their machines by selling spare parts at cost price and making technical information and diagnostics freely available to repairers. This makes their machines economic to repair and recondition after the guarantee period has run out, extending their life even further.

I believe we should build institutional support for longer life products, including among consumer groups, while presenting a convincing social, environmental and economic case and securing a change in consumer regulation.

Recommended resources

Evidence of consumer demand for retailer services on electrical products that offer alternatives to new product purchase, WRAP, 2013. http://www.wrap.org.uk/content/resource-efficient-business-models-consumer-research

Towards The Circular Economy - Economic and business rationale for an accelerated transition, Ellen MacArthur Foundation, 2012

A New Dynamic - effective business in a circular economy, Ellen MacArthur Foundation, 2013 (in press) – White Goods Case Study.

Chris Tuppen (British, born 1954) has been involved in sustainability for over twenty years. He runs Advancing Sustainability LLP and is an honorary professor at Keele University. He was previously BT's chief sustainability office.

Strategies for Resilience: Before You Save the World, Prepare to Save Yourself

Wayne Visser

The world has this nasty habit of changing without our permission; in fact, without us having so much as poked it in the eye. And so we – as individuals, organisations or whole nations – often find that we are no longer the agents of change, but rather its victims. Change happens! And we are left somewhere between mildly irritated and battling for our very survival.

According to Business Week, the average life expectancy of a Fortune 500 company is between 40 and 50 years. One-third of the Fortune 500 companies in existence in 1970 had vanished by 1983 – acquired, merged, or broken to pieces. Looking across the full spectrum of companies, large and small, the average life of companies may be as low as 12.5 years.

Can we really afford to talk about long-term sustainability, when short-term survival is so hard to achieve? The sobering fact is that we face a future in which saving the world may have to wait, while we save ourselves first. Chances are, we will even have to give up the smooth and swanky practice of sustainability, while we get down and dirty in the trenches of rough, rude resilience.

The bad news is that our silky green spandex outfits are probably not going to survive the trip. The good news is that resilience can be learned and planned for in advance. In a world of increasingly volatile sustainability challenges, there are five strategies for resilience that can dramatically increase our chances of survival when the waves of disruptive change come crashing in. They are to: defend, diversify, decentralize, dematerialize and define.

A *defensive strategy* can take on many forms, the most obvious of which is to insure against catastrophe, whatever form that may take. This only works if the crash is not systemic, but it is a good start. Other tactics include having a crack-squad of trouble-shooters trained to respond in times of crisis, and building up reserves for the proverbial rainy day, which may turn out to be a tsunami.

A *diversification strategy* applies to people, products and markets. For example, if you bet your corporate life on being a fossil fuel company, rather than an energy company, or if you are locked into a local market without any global investments, you are highly vulnerable. Likewise, if you hire an army of clones, your lack of diversity will leave you brittle in the face of change.

A *decentralization strategy* is based on the same rationale that inspired the Internet. By decentralising information and building in redundancy on local servers, the Internet is far less vulnerable to being 'taken out' in a single hit. In the same way, by decentralising operations, infrastructure and solutions – as with decentralised energy for example – we can be better prepared to cope with disruption.

A *dematerialization strategy* means moving to an industrial model that reduces dependency on resources. The only viable way to do this in the long term is to shift to renewable energy and to optimise the circular economy. Hence, anything we can do to decouple economic growth from environmental impacts is a step in the direction of greater resilience.

A *defining strategy* is about giving people a purpose to believe in. Victor Frankl, survivor of four Nazi concentration camps and psychiatric author of *Man's Search for Meaning*, gives compelling evidence that our resilience under extreme circumstances often comes down to having an existential belief about something worth living for. Can sustainability offer us this compelling cause?

By pursing these five resilience strategies, individuals, organisations and even countries will be much better placed to endure the creative destruction to come. However, preparing for change is not the same thing as surviving it. Resilience is not a strategy, but an ability – one which is shaped and tempered in the fire of extreme experience.

At its heart, this ability to be resilient is about adapting when everything around us is changing – like an aspen tree. Aspen forests are able to survive frequent avalanches that literally flatten them. The trees survive and spring back up because they have an interconnected network of underground roots and their trunks and branches are highly pliable.

The key message is that the secret to transformational change in the world is connectivity and dexterity. After all, Darwin never claimed that the fittest would survive, only the most adaptable.

Wayne Visser (South African, born 1970) is an author, social entrepreneur, speaker, researcher, and lecturer in future-fitness, sustainability, corporate social responsibility, and purpose-inspired business. He is director of the think tank consultancy Kaleidoscope Futures, founder of CSR International, Chair of Sustainable Business at the Gordon Institute of Business Science in South Africa and a Senior Associate at the University of Cambridge.

Ballyhoo Economic Risks of Overshoot

Mathis Wackernagel

If we could mark Ecological Deficit Days for each country that runs such a deficit with media campaigns on economic risk, we could significantly increase controversy and interest. The goal is to get countries (or more specifically their economic advisors) to call for advice.

One idea I fancy is to organize a class-action suit against US economics departments or business schools which promised students to prepare them for the world. They should be sued for damages because, in reality, they indoctrinated them with theories that are absolutely contradictory to physical reality – the ideology of infinite growth. Who would be the suing class? There are lots of students stuck with huge student loans and inadequate preparation for the world. Yet Universities have large endowments and mis-educated them. This could turn into a perfect storm and media spectacle: a perfect combination. Just imagine how this would spur wild opinions and what positions such a campaign could generate in public and private. OK, perhaps this is a bit too wild.

Let me now propose a more practical idea. It is built on the recognition that there is a great opportunity to communicate the economic risk of overshoot far more effectively than we have done before: mainly, by linking it to people's economic self interest.

Here's how. Global Footprint Network has started a campaign (inspired by Andrew Simms from the New Economics Foundation) to mark every year's Earth Overshoot Day. This is the day in the year by which, on aggregate, humanity has demanded as much from the Earth as the Earth can renew in the entire year. In 2013, this day fell on 20 August. This is what we calculate with our Ecological Footprint accounts, by comparing how much bio-productive space is needed for the human endeavor, compared to how much is available on the planet. If demand exceeds supply, then we are in overshoot.

This year's campaign was the most successful so far – with 240 million people potentially reading the story on Internet, endless radio and media reports, plus a few TV stories. 'La Stampa' had Earth Overshoot Day as the main graphic feature on their front page.

We were more successful this year because we made a small shift in our communication. Rather than reporting how many planets it takes if everybody lived like a Swiss, an American or a Japanese person, we reported how many Switzerlands it takes to support Switzerland (about 4), or how many Americas to support the Americans (about 2), etc.

Now, the idea is to extend the campaign. Let's bring the focus to the national level and engage ecological creditor countries. 85% of the world population that lives in a country that runs a bio-capacity deficit, i.e. demands more from nature than their ecosystems can renew. Select perhaps about 20 of them and run, in addition to the Ecological Overshoot Day, each country's Ecological Deficit Day. Switzerland, using about four times more than what it has, would mark this day around March 30.

Using strong local media partners, the day would be used to develop a risk profile for the country that economic analysts of the country could easily understand and interpret. It would be done with a media and Internet campaign that highlights this risk assessment with statistics, tidbits of information and rich info-graphs. All attractively designed.

Figure 7: Ecological Deficits by Country

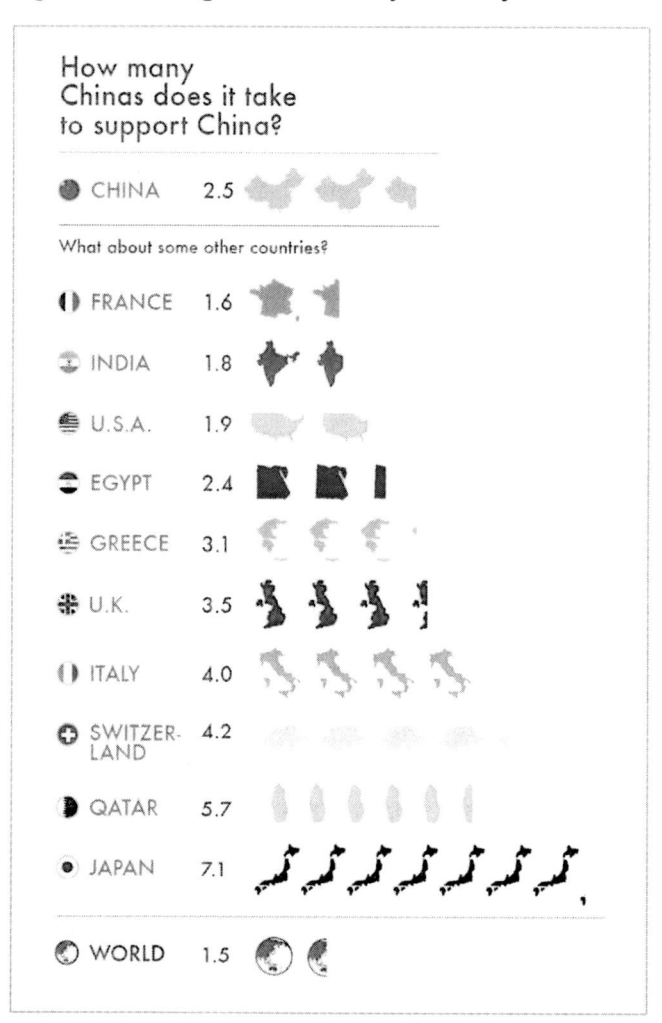

How many Chinas does it take to support China?

● CHINA	2.5	

What about some other countries?

◐ FRANCE	1.6	
◉ INDIA	1.8	
◈ U.S.A.	1.9	
◉ EGYPT	2.4	
◈ GREECE	3.1	
✤ U.K.	3.5	
◐ ITALY	4.0	
✚ SWITZERLAND	4.2	
◗ QATAR	5.7	
◉ JAPAN	7.1	
◯ WORLD	1.5	

Source: Global Footprint Network, 2013

The risk assessment would explore:

- What are the implications of the bio-capacity and Footprint trends for the competitiveness of the country?
- What are the current resource costs, and how have they changed?
- What are the weak-points of the country's energy system and what are realistic alternatives to overcome the gaps?
- What does food security look like, considering trends in the country's main trading partners (who themselves are moving towards larger biocapacity deficits)?
- How could this risk affect the country's credit worthiness and competitiveness?

Hopefully, we could develop this information package as a double page for the country's key business newspapers (perhaps in collaboration with a key think-tank of that country, or an opinion leader), with supplementary stories for other news outlets.

Success would be measured by how many national governments call us afterwards for advice on how to address their resource risks. We hope for at least five countries to call after running this campaign for three years, plus many calls from large investors and asset owners (such as pension funds).

My question to you all is: are you interested in participating? We need help framing risks for countries you know (or live in), writing glimpses, advising on who should be media partners (we still have not fundraised for the idea, but are about to).

Recommended Resources

On the Overshoot Day Concept:
http://www.footprintnetwork.org/en/index.php/GFN/page/earth_overshoot_day/

Press Reaction for 2013:
http://www.footprintnetwork.org/en/index.php/GFN/blog/earth_overshoot_day_2013_around_the_world

Resource risks for sovereign bond investors:
http://www.footprintnetwork.org/en/index.php/GFN/page/environmental_risk_in_sovereign_credits_e-risc

---

Mathis Wackernagel (Swiss, born 1962) is cocreator of the ecological footprint concept and president of Global Footprint Network, an international sustainability think tank, with officesin Oakland, California; Geneva, Switzerland; and Brussels, Belgium.

Addressing the Underlying Systemic Issues

Karl Wagner

The idea that I want to share is the notion that we all should not shy away from our global challenges, but engage in trying to change things on the meta-level of systemic issues. It is not only possible; it also is the future.

It is becoming more and more evident that the various challenges or crises humanity faces are in fact aspects of one single systemic crisis. Unemployment, inequality, financial crises, biodiversity depletion, degradation of ecosystems and life-support systems, climate change – you name it, they are all related to an outdated worldview and a theory and practice of economics that has become counter-productive and detrimental for our future. This worldview has served us well for many years, but will need to be replaced with a new one if human society wants to transit into a sustainable and happier future on the planet.

Systemic issues can be seen as a hierarchical matrix where all levels are interconnected, or a holistic picture whereby each part contains the entire picture. These issues reach deep down in our biological make-up, where we find drivers as old as the biology of our hormone system or the evolution of our brain functions and capabilities. Added to this is the level of values, which guide our behaviour, and belief systems, which largely shape our perceptions of what we consider to be "the reality".

Worldviews are changing as society evolves and today's dominant belief systems (at least in the West, which has been influencing the rest of the world for many years) originate from the period of enlightenment. Unfortunately, what had started out as humanistic ideas with the wellbeing of the community in mind, has been distorted over the last couple of hundreds years and so we find ourselves in a world where competition is more important than cooperation; where material values trump over non-material ones; where caring for the community has been replaced by excessive individualism; and where liberty of mind has turned into the freedom of overconsumption and selfishness.

On a societal level, economics and governance has, over the last few hundred years, determined to a large degree the course of society. Economics has morphed into today's material-driven, wasteful consumer society and a 1% versus 99% world. Democracy, while still the best political system around, has accumulated so many deficiencies that its capabilities to properly guide the development of human society has severely suffered.

The dynamics of our economy (and its associated environmental degradation, depletion, overconsumption, inequality, poverty, etc.) is upheld through specific tools and methods, such as the focus on GDP as a measure of progress of human society equivalent to sales of goods and services, or the lack of properly valuing of natural resources. At the end of the chain of consequences, we find all the effects of a system gone wrong, ranging from climate change to poverty.

If one wants to develop a pragmatic action plan to tackle the underlying drivers of these negative developments, where to start? On the one hand, as systemic issues are systemic and interrelated, any topic can serve as point of entry into the matrix. On the other hand, it is also obvious that the most powerful and decisive driver behind what's going wrong is the prevailing economics. No matter which negative global development we want to stop, correct and alter, in the end we will have to replace our current economic system with a new one. Economics interacts with every person just about every day and it is a root cause behind every single crisis humanity faces on a global level.

The outlines of the new economy have become fairly visible and there is little doubt amongst a growing number of people, including economists and enlightened politicians, about the direction that it needs to take:

- From a flow through economy to a circular economy;
- From a quantitative material concept of growth to a qualitative one;
- From an economy which serves fewer and fewer to one which serves a maximum of people;
- From efficiency through more machines to more jobs for real people;
- From more production to maintenance and repair;
- From consumer to earth citizen; and
- A regulatory framework, which makes sure, that the finance industry serves the economy and the economy serves the majority of people.

The new ideas are there and more and more people from all walks of life sense or understand emotionally, intuitively and intellectually the need to change economics and the direction we are taking. The failings of the current economics are becoming more and more self-evident, day-by-day.

Disrupting the Future

A movement is already in the making, but those who benefit from the current system and do not want any change – plus all those who are wedded to the old worldview and cannot find their way out of it – effectively build a barrier against natural change happening. They force humanity directly and indirectly to stay on a detrimental course of rising inequality and looming social unrest, rising CO_2 concentrations, waste and resource depletion. Hundreds of billions of dollars are spent to maintain the old worldview through propaganda, PR, advertising and lobbying of opinion-makers and decision-makers.

What stops us from trying to change this by addressing economics? Would this not be the most sensible thing to do? Are there not millions of concerned and educated people who ultimately have created and are funding thousands of civil society organizations whose task it ought to be to make the world a better, safer and more stabile place?

What evidently stops us is the magnitude of the task as changing the global system of economics seems too big too handle, too nebulous and fuzzy and outright unrealistic and impossible. But what's wrong with trying? Does this not have more to do with attitude, spirit, uncorrupted idealism, guts and vision of those who could make a difference than with the complexity of the task?

Have we – as individuals, as representatives of civil society and as concerned citizens – lost the vision and drive to tackle the real issues no matter how big they are? Are we all too much part of the system we would like to change and therefore unable to confront it fundamentally? Are we too concerned about growing in material terms ourselves - as individuals, organizations, institutions and businesses? Have we become a schizophrenic people, who intellectually understand perfectly well what would need to be done, while in daily life we are the ordinary hamster in the running wheel, having to run faster and faster just to stay in the same place?

If the apparent complexity is our challenge, then why not try to find a way through this complexity, which allows us to find clear and pragmatic lines of action and to change the global economic system as the key driver behind the global challenges we face?

This is the basic goal behind a process I have been invited to lead for several foundations concerned that they invest many millions of dollars into winning a war, while all they do is win skirmishes and a battle here or there. A first phase with initial concrete answers will be completed end of 2013.

The process made me understand, that

1. There is a powerful movement building up. The wave is forming and it will be about surfing the wave and not about creating it.
2. We should not be afraid of tackling the real drivers and the big, fundamental issues; it is after all the right and most sensible thing to do.
3. It is possible to devise clear targets, strategies and action plans to address   underlying systemic issues
4. It will be about small actions taken by millions of 'normal' people.
5. It will be about small businesses and short distances.
6. It will also be about civil society overcoming self-built barriers, which focus their attention on the wellbeing of their organizations rather than on the wellbeing of the planet and its inhabitants.

Karl Wagner (Austrian, born 1952), biologist by education and environmental campaigner by training, has spent thirty years running environmental campaigns, nationally and globally, mostly for the World Wildlife Fund. He currently works for the Club of Rome.

The Soil Carbon Olympics

Peter Willis

The idea is to hold a global competition every four years to identify, applaud and profile farmers who have sequestered the most carbon in their soil during the preceding period. In true Olympic fashion, medals and renown would go to winners in various categories.

Why? When land is farmed with soil health and carbon content as key goals, its soil can store vast amounts of atmospheric CO2 in the form of carbon, and over relatively short time periods. Set alongside the more traditionally favoured tree-planting, the strategy of sequestering carbon in soil through specific faming approaches (e.g. Holistic Management for livestock and 'no-till' for arable land) has the advantage that it raises soil fertility and therefore food production, and in turn rural employment, all with little reliance on chemical fertilisers and pesticides. Soil carbon also appears to stay in the soil for longer than carbon sequestered in trees, which typically die or are burnt within 30-80 years. So it has the potential to be a big 'win-win' strategy.

However, agricultural orthodoxy still holds sway and tends not to recognise the value of farming in this way. It is time that the evident success of those pioneering farmers who are adopting this approach was given much greater recognition. They are the nodes in the small but growing global movement – mainly at present to be found in Australia, North America and South Africa. Farmers, being very practical people, learn best from observing other farmers' successes, so broadcasting the stories and the data on improved farm outcomes seems like a good idea.

The Soil Carbon Olympics (SCO) would be run virtually – no expensive stadia are required! A Soil Carbon Olympics Board would be convened, which would have representation from experienced soil and climate scientists, holistic farming experts and the sponsors (see below). The Board would in turn appoint a small Organising Committee to manage the SCO. The Organising committee would send out the competition rules and all other information to farming communities worldwide and then receive entries at the due time, organise adjudication and manage the announcement of winners, despatch of medals and all the surrounding publicity.

The awards ceremony would be held in a different farming town somewhere in the world every four years, using cutting edge technology to beam in winning farmers and show video clips of their farming approaches and their winning statistics. Medals would be presented by globally prominent climate change and farming 'personalities'.

Soil carbon would be measured in the standard way via soil samples that are taken annually from competing farms, analysed in laboratories and verified by approved auditing firms, representatives of which would need to oversee collection and testing of all the soil samples. Technology for measuring soil carbon is advancing and portable devices are being developed (using either laser or near-infrared spectroscopy) that mean analysis can be done swiftly and relatively cheaply.[13]

---

[13] See http://cgspace.cgiar.org/bitstream/handle/10568/10279/ccafs-wp-02-soil_carbon_measurement.pdf?sequence=5 for discussion of these technical advances.

It is hoped that one of the Big Four global auditing firms would see this as an opportunity not only to be associated with an initiative with serious potential to reduce atmospheric carbon and improve farm productivity, but also to provide high-quality business leads amongst some of the world's more far-sighted (and productive) farmers. This hope is based on the enthusiasm shown at an earlier stage (2008) by the South African Institute of Chartered Accountants, for these two very reasons.

In researching this idea, I have re-ignited both my bafflement that the potential of carbon sequestration in soil is so widely ignored by farmers, scientists and governments around the world, and my enthusiasm to change that. If anyone is interested to join me – and the sprinkling of other advocates for a soil carbon revolution around the world – do let me know!

Recommended Resources

Amazing Carbon: www.amazingcarbon.com (based in Australia)

Jones, C. (2010) Soil carbon - can it save agriculture's bacon? Agriculture & Greenhouse Emissions Conference, May 2010.

Savory, A. (2013) How to green the world's deserts and reverse climate change, TED Talk.

Soil Carbon Coalition: www.soilcarboncoalition.org (based in North America).

Peter Willis (South African, born 1954) is the South African director of the Cambridge Programme for Sustainability Leadership and regional chairman of the Prince of Wales's Business & Sustainability

Programme. After a history degree from Oxford he worked in government and started various enterprises before emigrating to South Africa in 1993.